Fed by
God's Grace

D1377827

Fed by God's Grace

COMMUNION PRAYERS for

Year B

Michael E. Dixon
Sandy Dixon

Chalice Press
St. Louis, Missouri

ixon

duced without
written permis..... , St. Louis, MO
63166-0179.

All scripture quotations, unless otherwise indicated, are from the
New Revised Standard Version Bible, copyright 1989, Division of Chris-
tian Education of the National Council of Churches of Christ in the
USA. Used by permission.

Cover design: Elizabeth Wright
Cover art: Detail from window by Francis Deck at St. Agnes Church,
    Springfield, Ill. Photo © The Crosiers
Interior design: Elizabeth Wright

Visit Chalice Press on the World Wide Web at
www.chalicepress.com

10 9 8 7 6 5 4 3 2 1   99 00 01 02 03 04

Library of Congress Cataloging–in–Publication Data

(Pending)

Printed in the United States of America

Contents

Introduction

The table is ready. Worshipers gather. We sing, we pray, we hear the Word. We are invited to come to the table, to eat and drink, to do as Christ's disciples did in the upper room long ago. And we pray. The spoken prayers of the leaders mingle with the unspoken prayers of the community. Then, by the grace of God, we are spiritually fed.

Fed by God's Grace: Communion Prayers for Year B is one of three books planned for those of you who are called upon to pray aloud at Christ's table. We hope that these prayers will serve as promptings, models, or clues to give you input as you prepare your own prayers. If they stimulate your thoughts, sharpen your insights, and focus your attention, they will serve their purpose. If, on some Sundays, you want to use the prayers as written here, adopting these words as your own, that's all right too.

Many previous books of communion prayers have followed a single model, such as separate prayers for the bread and the cup. *Fed by God's Grace* offers more models. For each Sunday, you will find four prayers: one for the bread, one for the cup, a unified prayer for both bread and cup, and a closing prayer to be used after the communion service. That way, you can choose the model that fits your situation.

We offer these suggestions on how to prepare for praying at the Lord's table.

- If your congregation uses the Revised Common Lectionary, check to see what Sunday of the church year you will be praying, then find the appropriate page in this book.

- If your congregation doesn't use the Revised Common Lectionary, it may follow the general seasons of the church year. Find a set of prayers appropriate to the season.
- If your congregation doesn't use the Revised Common Lectionary and you want to choose a prayer that connects with the scripture lesson for the day, use the Scripture Index in the back of the book.
- When you have selected a prayer, read and reflect on all the scripture readings at the top of the page. This is a part of your spiritual preparation for serving at the table, as well as helping you understand the concepts behind the prayer.
- Read the prayer to yourself (and to God), as spiritual preparation and rehearsal. Revise the prayer as necessary to fit your own beliefs or those of your congregation or denomination and to fit any particular contexts of your local situation. Write out the prayer, make notes, or commit it to memory, as is right for you.
- Before the service begins, take a few moments of silent prayer and reflection or take time to pray together with others who are leading worship.

As mentioned above, these collections of prayers for the communion table follow the seasons of the church year. The church year begins with Advent, the season of preparation before Christmas. From there we move into Epiphany, Lent, Eastertide, and finally Pentecost, the longest season of the church year. The Revised Common Lectionary, a three-year cycle of scripture readings increasingly being used in many congregations, follows a progression of scripture passages designed to give the minister and congregation an overview of the Bible: Hebrew scriptures, psalms, epistles, and gospels. For year A, the major gospel is Matthew; year B, Mark; and year C, Luke. All three years use John.

Prayers in these books will pick their eucharistic themes from the scriptures. Not every scripture is used in each Sunday's sets of prayers, but we tried to touch base with the themes, if not the words, of each set of scripture texts.

We have used as our source of scripture listings the volume that was published in 1992, *The Revised Common Lectionary*, developed by the Consultation on Common Texts. Following the lectionary plan, this book has built in all the variables for the calendar years. Confusingly, not all the seasons are the same length from year to year. Lent counts backward from the date of Easter, and Pentecost falls seven Sundays after Easter. Since Easter moves, that means that Epiphany may be very short and Pentecost very long in a given year, or that Epiphany will be longer and Pentecost shorter in another year. You might want to check with the pastor to see what Sunday of the church year you will be serving at the table.

As we were nearing the completion of this volume of prayers, under some pressure to get it finished, needing all the time we possibly could schedule, several crises entered our lives. Sandy's mother suffered a stroke and passed away; Mike's dad had health problems at the same time, filling us with great uncertainty. We were in a town more than 300 miles from our home to be with Sandy's family; we were more than 1,000 miles from Mike's dad's home. It was a difficult time, to say the least.

Yet, over and over, the title of this series became real to us. "Fed by God's grace" took on meaning as we experienced the grace of God revealed to us in God's people. The ministers who were with us offered prayers, renewed and made new friendships, and through the funeral service read the word of eternal life. The many friends in many places who prayed for our parents and the family members who were physically present to witness the service of resurrection truly were feeding us by God's grace.

For this, we offer thanksgiving as the first book is completed.

First Sunday of Advent

Isaiah 64:1–9
Psalm 80:1–7, 17–19
1 Corinthians 1:3–9
Mark 13:24–37

PRAYER FOR THE BREAD: O God, who gives us life anew, help us this Advent season to be aware of the signs of your coming. Come into our lives afresh, mold us into the beings you would have us be. As we share this bread, the symbol of the body of your Son, the Christ, let it nourish our spirits. Let us truly be and do the work of Your hands. Amen.

PRAYER FOR THE CUP: Our God, as we continue in the feast set before us, help us remember that in the waiting for the Advent, the coming of your Son, Jesus, we are strengthened in the knowledge of your faithfulness to us. This cup before us is the visible reminder of that faithfulness, the blood of Jesus Christ given for us. As we wait for the coming, let us drink in thanksgiving for the gift that awaits us. Amen.

UNIFIED PRAYER: Into a world of noise and confusion, you will come to us quietly, Lord Jesus, as a child. Into a world of darkness, you will bring light. Into a world of greediness and desire, you will come as the perfect gift— the gift of love from our Creator. Into a world filled with hunger and thirst, you will give us bread and wine, so we will never have to spiritually hunger or thirst. As we wait for the coming of the Christ, let us take the bread and cup, remembering that sacrifice made in love for us. Fed and refreshed, we thank you, our Savior, for life anew. Amen.

PRAYER AFTER COMMUNION: In the silence we have come to hear your voice, dear God. The elements of communion that we have shared have reminded us of the one for whom we prepare. Help us to find your Spirit's presence and hear your voice in every day of this Advent season. Amen.

Second Sunday of Advent

Isaiah 40:1–11
Psalm 85:1–2, 8–13
2 Peter 3:8–15a
Mark 1:1–8

PRAYER FOR THE BREAD: We wait eagerly for your coming, God. During the season of Advent, the anticipation is hard. Yet even during the waiting, we confess that our lives do not always reflect Christlike ways. The ways of the world are much too easy. Forgive us when we sin; help us to lead lives of righteousness. When we eat the bread, the symbol of the body of Jesus Christ, we are committing ourselves to leading lives worthy of salvation in you. Make our paths straight as we wait for your coming. Amen.

PRAYER FOR THE CUP: O wonderful God, we come to your table this Advent day in praise for what you have done for us. You have cared for your people through the generations; your word of salvation has been promised to your heirs.

And now, through the life, ministry, and even death of your son, Jesus Christ, that promise is fulfilled in his resurrection. This cup is the symbol of that promise. Let us drink from it in praise! Amen.

UNIFIED PRAYER:

> Comfort, comfort you my people;
> tell of peace, thus says our God;
> comfort those who sit in darkness
> bowed beneath oppression's load.
> Speak you to Jerusalem
> of the peace that waits for them;
> tell them that their sins I cover;
> and their warfare now is over.

> Make you straight what long was crooked,
> make the rougher places plain;
> let your hearts be true and humble,
> as befits God's holy reign.
> For the glory of our God
> now o'er earth is shed abroad;
> and all flesh shall see the token
> that God's word is never broken.*

The body and blood of God's son, Jesus Christ; the bread and cup on this table are the token of God's word—never broken. Let us eat and drink, comforted by the love of our God. Amen.

PRAYER AFTER COMMUNION: We are sad to leave this table, dear God, for these moments were dear to us. Yet we rejoice, because we know that in the living Christ you are Immanuel—God with us—and we can find your presence everywhere. Amen.

*Johannes G. Olearius, "Comfort, Comfort You My People."

Third Sunday of Advent

Isaiah 61:1–4, 8–11
Psalm 126 or *Luke 1:47–55*
1 Thessalonians 5:16–24
John 1:6–8, 19–28

PRAYER FOR THE BREAD: Through many ages, God, you have been faithful to your people. You have rescued us many times from oppression and injustice. You have given us hope in a world in which despair too often is prevalent. Yet, even more, you have given us your covenant of love, salvation in Jesus Christ. The bread we eat this day is the reminder of this salvation. Let us rejoice.

PRAYER FOR THE CUP: We rejoice this Advent season as we celebrate at the table. Our hearts are filled with praise and song as we prepare for your coming again into the world. O God of salvation, as we drink this cup, let us celebrate your powerful love for us: love so powerful that you would bring your son into the world for us. We rejoice as we participate together in remembering your love. Amen.

UNIFIED PRAYER: Into a world filled with discord and injustice, oppression and bondage, hopelessness and despair, you have come, Lord. In this season of Advent, we hear the good news of salvation and hope. Because of your coming, we can sing praises in your name. This bread and cup before us are the fulfillment of the promise to your people, the symbols of a risen Savior. Let us share these emblems together, receiving the power to embody the liberating spirit of your Son, Jesus Christ.

PRAYER AFTER COMMUNION: In Christ is our joy. In Christ is our hope. In Christ you are present with us, O God of love. At this table, we have come in faith to eat with the living Christ. We bless you and thank you for the joy, the hope, and the presence of Christ we have experienced here. Amen.

Fourth Sunday of Advent

2 Samuel 7:1–11, 16
Luke 1:47–55 or *Psalm 89:1–4, 19–26*
Romans 16:25–27
Luke 1:26–38

PRAYER FOR THE BREAD: O God of mystery and surprise, we think of Mary, a poor country woman who baked bread for her family. How faithful she was to accept your promise and to accept the awesome responsibility of bearing the Christ. The infant that grew in her womb would grow up to be the living bread, Jesus the Christ. As we eat this bread, we remember a mother's self-giving love, a love that her son—your son—would make perfect. Lead us on the path of trust and love as we follow your Spirit. Amen.

PRAYER FOR THE CUP: May glory be yours, O wise and true God, forever and ever! You have disclosed to all the world the mystery of your love, so that people all over the world might respond in faith. As we prepare our hearts to celebrate the birth of Jesus the Christ, the one who discloses your way, we come to his table. We come to lift a cup, to bless it and drink from it, and thus to unite our hearts with Christ and with one another. As Mary looked ahead to her son's birth, as Christ looked ahead to the cross and the resurrection victory, help us to look ahead to your promised reign. Let Christ's spirit be born in us. Amen.

UNIFIED PRAYER: It's Christmastime, Jesus, and all over the world people are magnifying your great name, singing magnificats to you, and coming to your house to worship you more often. It's as if you are a celebrity!

We'll have to admit, Jesus, that sometimes we want to make you a celebrity. Maybe if we lift you up high enough, we'll forget that when you were here on earth in the flesh, you walked with men and women who had broken lives and dirt under their fingernails. Maybe if we make you a big enough celebrity, we can keep you as our healing, loving, miraculous Savior and won't hear you asking us to walk, work, and witness among those with broken lives and dirt under their fingernails. Maybe if we focus on your shining light, we won't see our own broken lives and dirty fingernails.

Everpresent Jesus, at this table and through these elements of bread and wine, reveal your whole self to us. Set our feet on a path that leads us not to a celebrity Jesus but to a brilliant star—a star that shines over a manger and causes us to kneel in humble adoration and praise for the one whose starlight shines into every darkness with hope and peace.

With starlight in our eyes and dirt under our fingernails, we pray. Amen.*

PRAYER AFTER COMMUNION: Our souls magnify you, O God, because you have done great things. Holy is your name. You always remember your children with grace and mercy, and you have given us this communion meal as an emblem of your love. Thank you for the precious gift of Jesus Christ. Amen.

*Contributed by Ben Bohren.

Christmas Eve / Christmas Day

Isaiah 9:2–7	*Isaiah 62:6–12*	*Isaiah 52:7–10*
Psalm 96	*Psalm 97*	*Psalm 98*
Titus 2:11–14	*Titus 3:4–7*	*Hebrews 1:1–4 (5–12)*
Luke 2:1–14	*Luke 2:(1–7)*	*John 1:1–14*
(15–20)	*8–20*	

(Any of the above scriptures may be used on
Christmas Eve or Christmas Day)

PRAYER FOR THE BREAD:

"How silently, how silently
the wondrous gift is given!
So God imparts to human hearts
The joys of highest heaven."*

On this Christmas eve, we come to your table, O God of Light, in awe of the miracle of the birth of your son, Jesus Christ Especially on this night, we are made aware of your great love for each of us.

"No ear may hear Christ coming,
But in this world of sin,
where meek souls will receive him still,
The dear Christ enters in."*

At this table we share the gift also of this bread, the body of your Son. Thank you for the forgiveness of our sins, and your presence in our lives. Enter our lives again tonight as together we share this bread in celebration of Jesus Christ. Amen.

*Phillips Brooks, "O Little Town of Bethlehem."

PRAYER FOR THE CUP:

> "Ah, dearest Jesus, holy Child,
> make thee a bed, soft, undefiled,
> within my heart, that it may be
> a quiet chamber kept for thee."*

Within our hearts, O God, make a place for your Son, that we may keep his name before us in all that we do. On this very special night of nights, taking the cup that is the blood of your new covenant has renewed meaning for us. The manger leads to the cross, the cross to new life. We praise you for this wondrous gift. Let us glorify you. Amen.

UNIFIED PRAYER: Loving God, we come to you in this decorated sanctuary, celebrating the birth of Jesus Christ, our Lord and Savior. We gather at this table and we wonder. It seems like such a long distance from Bethlehem's manger to the upper room, to Calvary, to the empty tomb. Yet it is here that your love comes full circle. The love that gave us Mary's baby is the same love that gave us the teacher in the upper room who blessed the bread and the cup. Birth and death, life and new life are all one as you in Christ are one with us. Amen.

PRAYER AFTER COMMUNION: Immanuel, God with us. Always, forever, in our hearts and lives, we celebrate your coming this day. Let us go from this celebration of bread and cup doing as the angels sang, "Praising God and saying Glory to God in the highest." Amen.

---

*Martin Luther, "From Heaven Above to Earth I Come."

First Sunday after Christmas Day

Isaiah 61:10–62:3
Psalm 148
Galatians 4:4–7
Luke 2:22–40

PRAYER FOR THE BREAD: God of light, whose Christmas gift to your people has put out darkness, we thank you for the opportunity to come to your table today. As we break and eat this bread, let your everlasting light shine in our lives as we seek to follow the newly born, yet risen Christ. Amen.

PRAYER FOR THE CUP: Because you sent Jesus Christ into the world, we are called by a new name, O God. We are your people, Christ's people, redeemed and free. The cup we drink this morning is a sign of your grace, a sign of Christ's undying love. Help us realize as we drink from it the joy that comes from the presence of your Spirit. Amen.

UNIFIED PRAYER: At your table this day, we come in thanksgiving for the gift we have received this week. Along with the other gifts this Christmas, the gift that has come from you, God, surpasses anything else we could ever receive. Out of your great love for us you gave us your Son, our Savior Jesus Christ.

At this table we remember another gift you gave us—eternal life. We eat the bread and drink from the cup in humble gratitude for the magnitude of these gifts, remembering the sacrifice Jesus the Christ made so that we might have these gifts. Let us commune in the presence of the Holy Spirit. Amen.

PRAYER AFTER COMMUNION: We thank you for these moments of communion, O giving God, because they remind us what the Christmas season is all about: that you cared enough to send Jesus Christ into the world, that we might know your love. Amen.

Second Sunday after Christmas Day

Jeremiah 31:7–14
Psalm 147:12–20
Ephesians 1:3–14
John 1:(1–9), 10–18

PRAYER FOR THE BREAD: Creator God, you have given us, your chosen people, so much. We can scarcely begin to count all your gifts. We know you watch and care for us always. Your greatest gift to us is our Savior, Jesus Christ. Through him, we experience salvation and life forever with you. As we eat this loaf, reminding us of the body of Jesus Christ, we praise you with joy and gladness.

PRAYER FOR THE CUP: "Gracious Father, whose Son Jesus Christ is the eternal Word of power and glory: we give you thanks for this cup of blessing with which we remember Jesus, who lived among us full of grace and truth. Send your Spirit to this communion feast, so that as we drink this wine we may be nourished by Christ's own life, enlightened by Christ's own light, and inspired by Christ's own self. All this we ask in Jesus' name. Amen."*

*From *Thankful Praise* (St. Louis: CBP Press, 1987), 71.

UNIFIED PRAYER: We come to your table today, God, to share in a meal of justice. Your table is a global table, where all are welcome, where all are forgiven, where all are called into community with each other. Here we are given a vision—rooted in hope—of what you intend for all humankind. Here we eat the bread of justice. We drink the cup of the new covenant and are liberated from the fears that have driven us to exclude, devalue and dominate others. We are nourished to be more open, more just, more loving, and to walk in friendship with God and each other. From this meal, we go forth not in despair, but in this Christmastide, we go in hope.*

PRAYER AFTER COMMUNION: Let us taste and see how good the Redeemer is. With loving hearts, with hope-filled faith, with deeds of justice, may we live in doxology—offering praise and thanksgiving for God's lavish, persistent, and redeeming love. Amen.*

*Adapted from Ronice Branding, *Fulfilling the Dream* (St. Louis: Chalice Press, 1998), 133f.

First Sunday after Epiphany

Genesis 1:1–5
Psalm 29
Acts 19:1–7
Mark 1:4–11

PRAYER FOR THE BREAD: Creator God, you have revealed yourself to us in many ways. Yours are the great gifts of creation that make life possible. From the wheat that helps sustain life, your children have made bread. The bread that we now break reminds us of another way you have revealed yourself to us, in the life and ministry, death and resurrection of Jesus Christ. Bless us by your Spirit as we eat this bread, that we may be aware that you are the giver of all good gifts. Amen.

PRAYER FOR THE CUP: We have heard your voice, O God, for you are the God who calls your children to yourself. We respond to your voice, because we trust in your love. The cup we now raise reminds us of your beloved Son, Jesus Christ, who came to us that we might know for ourselves your ways of love. Guide us on those ways by your Spirit. Amen.

UNIFIED PRAYER: You are the God of light; you are the God of life; you are the God of love. As this season of Epiphany begins, we reflect on how beautifully your light, life, and love are revealed in our Savior, Jesus Christ. As we come to this table to eat the bread and drink from the cup, let the light of Christ illumine our minds, let the life of Christ give us new life, and let the love of Christ transform our hearts. Empowered by your Spirit, we pray. Amen.

PRAYER AFTER COMMUNION: In Jesus Christ your word has become deed. At this table we have affirmed your love made real to us in Jesus Christ. Now help us to go and make your love real to others. Amen.

Second Sunday after Epiphany

1 Samuel 3:1–10 (11–20)
Psalm 139:1–6, 13–18
1 Corinthians 6:12–20
John 1:43–51

PRAYER FOR THE BREAD: As we gather at your table, Lord, the words of the scripture are fresh in our minds. We have heard God calling Samuel; we have heard Jesus calling the disciples. You call each of us in different ways to be your people, to do your work. As we share the bread, the visible symbol of Jesus' body, the visible symbol of your great love for us, help us to know your call for us.

As we eat this bread, call us to find ways of sharing the bread with others—spiritually and physically. Let us take the bread, eat, and hear your words for us. Amen.

PRAYER FOR THE CUP: You have searched us and you know us, O Creator God. You formed us to share your love. Yet we so often ignore your presence in our lives. Help open our eyes to the mystery of your love. At this communion table help us find a sign of that great love. As we bless and drink this wine, fill our hearts with a sense of the presence of our Lord Jesus Christ. By your Spirit we pray. Amen.

UNIFIED PRAYER: Eternal God, you have formed us in love, you watch over us in love, you lovingly call us to faithful discipleship. As we eat this bread and drink this cup, we thank you for your eternal loving-kindness, best revealed to us in our Savior, Jesus Christ. As we partake of this meal, open our ears to better hear your word, open our eyes to better see the world's needs, open our hearts, that we may serve you. Let us walk in your Spirit always. Amen.

PRAYER AFTER COMMUNION: For the gift of life and light, we thank you. For the elements of which we have partaken, we thank you. For the love of Jesus Christ that we lift up here today, we thank you. For your Spirit's presence in our daily lives, we thank you. Amen.

Third Sunday after Epiphany

Jonah 3:1–5, 10
Psalm 62:5–12
1 Corinthians 7:29–31
Mark 1:14–20

PRAYER FOR THE BREAD: You are our rock and salvation, O God, our refuge and strength. As this community of believers gathers at the table, we sometimes feel over-whelmed by the pressures and crises of daily life. But here in the silence, as we reflect upon the love of our Lord Jesus Christ, as we pour out our hearts to you in prayer, we find the strength we need. As we break this bread, we share in the meaning of Christ's sacrifice and come to trust your steadfast love. In your Spirit's name we pray. Amen.

PRAYER FOR THE CUP: In Jesus Christ, we have heard your call to follow. As did Simon and Andrew, we have re-sponded. We call ourselves Christ's disciples. Help us learn from Christ the meaning of love, the meaning of service. Help us learn from this cup the meaning of sac-rifice, the meaning of covenant. When we would falter or wander away, send your Spirit to guide us back to faithfulness. In the name of the faithful Christ we pray. Amen.

UNIFIED PRAYER: O God, who has a purpose for each of us, we have heard the call of Jonah. We have heard the call Jesus gave to each of his disciples. In our lives, we too hear your call. Help us know your power and love as we respond to your call. As we eat this bread and drink from this cup, forgive us the times we ignored your voice. Let the nourishment from this holy meal give us courage and strength to respond to your call. Amen.

PRAYER AFTER COMMUNION: As we leave this table, O Lord of love, let the memories of these moments sustain and guide us, so that in the weeks ahead we may never forget whose we are. Amen.

Fourth Sunday after Epiphany

Deuteronomy 18:15–20
Psalm 111
1 Corinthians 8:1–13
Mark 1:21–28

PRAYER FOR THE BREAD: Gracious and merciful God, we gather as a congregation to praise you, to give you thanks, and to receive your blessing. As you have provided food for our tables, you provide us with this spiritual food, this bread that we break now, to signify our covenant with Jesus Christ. In Jesus Christ, you have sent us redemption. Let his praise endure forever. Amen.

PRAYER FOR THE CUP: In your word, O God, is truth. Your word guided Moses and the prophets to keep faith alive. Your word took on flesh in Jesus Christ, who healed and taught and showed us your way. The cup we now drink confirms the covenant that we have with you through Christ Jesus, a covenant of peace and love. We bless you and praise you for this cup and this covenant. Amen.

UNIFIED PRAYER: In a world filled with things that tempt but do not satisfy, that appeal but do not nourish, we come to your table to receive the elements of communion that fill our lives with richness and meaning. As we eat this bread and drink from this cup, let your Spirit so fill and strengthen us that we will know the presence of the living Christ in our lives and seek to serve him in all our days.

PRAYER AFTER COMMUNION: Your table has been spread; the bread has been broken and shared; the cup has been poured and blessed. Again, we have celebrated the communion that marks our covenant with the Lord Jesus Christ. We bless you and praise you for this transforming gift and for your Spirit's presence. Amen.

Fifth Sunday after Epiphany

Isaiah 40:21–31
Psalm 147:1–11, 20c
1 Corinthians 9:16–23
Mark 1:29–39

PRAYER FOR THE BREAD: Because we have heard your good news, O Loving God, we come to worship. Because your Spirit has called us, we have responded. Because Christ has invited us to this table, we come now to break bread. We remember now the Christ who called, who healed, who proclaimed your love, and who gave himself that we might have life. Bless us in your Spirit as we are fed by your grace. Amen.

PRAYER FOR THE CUP: We continue in prayer, dear God, asking that your blessing be upon this cup. Thank you for the wonderful gift of communion. Help us recall the wonderful good news of Jesus Christ and the gospel he gave us. Help us to be responsible and responsive stewards of that gospel. Refresh our spirits and grant us your peace in Christ's name. Amen.

UNIFIED PRAYER: You are great, O Lord, and abundant in power; yet your tender love heals the brokenhearted and lifts up the downtrodden. You provide food for all creation and delight in what you have made. Now you have invited us to the table given us by your son, Jesus Christ, to feed us by your grace and love. Here we eat the bread that strengthens our spirits. Here we drink the cup that unites us in Christ's love. Here we bless you and praise you for the peace that your Spirit sends. Amen.

PRAYER AFTER COMMUNION: We came to your table needy; we go satisfied. We came to your table alienated; we leave in community. We have shared in the blessing of your gospel. Let your Spirit guide us in the week ahead, that we may share your gospel with others. Amen.

Sixth Sunday after Epiphany (Proper 1)

2 Kings 5:1–14
Psalm 30
1 Corinthians 9:24–27
Mark 1:40–45

PRAYER FOR THE BREAD: God of mercy, you have been with us in our deepest moments of suffering and grief. We have known sorrow, but you have guided us beyond the sorrow to joy. As we gather to take and eat the bread of communion, we remember both the sorrow and the joy of the upper room, for it prefigured the sorrow of the cross and the joy of the empty tomb. The bread we eat is an expression of your grace. Let the lives we live be expressions of our joy and thankfulness for these holy moments. Guide us by your Spirit, we pray. Amen.

PRAYER FOR THE CUP: We come to this table, O God of love, knowing that here we can experience your presence. We do not feel worthy, but we know that your love makes us worthy. The cup we now drink calls us to affirm the covenant of your love; a love poured out for us in the healing life and sacrificial death of our Lord Jesus Christ. Let your love work within us as individuals and among us as a congregation, that we may truly be your witnesses. Amen.

UNIFIED PRAYER: We so often center our lives on our own selves and our own needs, dear God. Help us here at this communion table to center our lives on you. Help us realize that you are the living center. Help us learn the disciplines of prayer and listening so that we may call upon you and trust that you will listen. In the quietness of these communion moments, help us focus not on our worries and distractions, but on your presence. Let the bread and the wine that we now share strengthen our spirits. Let your healing presence work in the sore spots and open wounds of our lives. Let us know your peace. Let us receive the gift of your Spirit, as Christ has promised. Amen.

PRAYER AFTER COMMUNION: Let our souls praise you, O God, let our hearts not be silent. Let us forever give thanks to you for this feast of the Spirit. Amen.

Seventh Sunday after Epiphany (Proper 2)

Isaiah 43:18–25
Psalm 41
2 Corinthians 1:18–22
Mark 2:1–12

PRAYER FOR THE BREAD: Faithful God, we gather at this table, wanting to be your faithful people. The bread we break reminds us that in Jesus Christ you have said yes to us, affirming us and accepting us in your love. As we eat this bread we say our yes to you, affirming our desire to live out the gospel of Christ. As we are fed here, help us be sensitive to those who are poor and hungry in this world and to share as you have shared with us. Let your Spirit guide us to live as Christ would have us live. Amen.

PRAYER FOR THE CUP: Generous God, we thank you with all our hearts. You have blessed your creation so richly, providing us with all we need. As we drink this cup of communion, we find ourselves welcomed into the presence of the living Christ. As you have given the cold waters of spring rains to nourish the ground and to satisfy all creation, so you have given us a chance to drink of the living water of faith in Jesus Christ our Savior. In drinking this cup we affirm that you have redeemed us, not because of our worthiness, but because of your own nature. We come to you drawn by your Spirit, and bless your holy name. Amen.

UNIFIED PRAYER: Gracious God, your people bless you from generation to generation. In baptism you have put your seal on us as your people. At your communion table you reaffirm the covenant you have made with us in Jesus Christ. Bless this bread that we now break, and bless this cup that we drink as we recommit ourselves to the good news. Give us your Spirit in our hearts as we now partake. Amen.

PRAYER AFTER COMMUNION: What wondrous love is this, O my soul? What wondrous love is this, that you, O God, would give us Jesus Christ to blot out our transgressions? What wondrous love is this, that we can share in this communion meal and experience the presence of the living Christ in our lives? What can we do but bless you and praise you? Amen.

Eighth Sunday after Epiphany (Proper 3)

Hosea 2:14–20
Psalm 103:1–13, 22
2 Corinthians 3:1–6
Mark 2:13–22

PRAYER FOR THE BREAD: We bless you, O God, with all our souls. You have forgiven us, healed us, redeemed us, and crowned us as your children. We celebrate your enduring love as we gather around this table. As we break this bread, we affirm that Christ gave his body for us. As we eat this bread, we accept your covenant of love as our gift to receive and our responsibility to share. Let your Spirit guide us on the paths of faithfulness. Amen.

PRAYER FOR THE CUP: Today we acknowledge your covenant, O God, a covenant of righteousness, justice, steadfast love, and mercy. The cup we now drink is a seal of that covenant, given us through the sacrifice of our Lord Jesus Christ. Help us through your Spirit to be faithful to that covenant, as you are faithful to us. In Jesus' name we pray. Amen.

UNIFIED PRAYER: We gather around this table rejoicing, dear God, because you have invited us to be a people of the new covenant. In eating this bread and drinking this cup, we accept this covenant and pray that it will become an ever deeper part of our lives. Let your Spirit transform us so that the gospel of Jesus Christ may be written on our hearts and so that it may shine through in our daily lives. Amen.

PRAYER AFTER COMMUNION: We have heard your call to follow Christ, and today we have shared at Christ's table as disciples and as friends. Help us to be faithful to this call and to this covenant that we have affirmed today. Amen.

Last Sunday after Epiphany

2 Kings 2:1–2
Psalm 50:1–6
2 Corinthians 4:3–6
Mark 9:2–9

PRAYER FOR THE BREAD: God of glory, God of light, in Jesus Christ we have seen your holiness. We know in faith that Jesus is your beloved Son. Bless us now by your Spirit as we break bread in Christ's name. Let Christ's Spirit live within us, that others might see in us your saving grace. Amen.

PRAYER FOR THE CUP: We have gathered, gracious God, as your faithful children. We have gathered to celebrate the covenant that was sealed by our Savior's blood. Bless this cup we drink, so that the light of Christ's life might shine through us. Guide us by your Spirit. Amen.

UNIFIED PRAYER: In the darkness of our despair and confusion, O God, you have said, "Let light shine out of darkness." Your light shines in our hearts, as we experience your glory in Jesus Christ. Bless this bread that we break and the cup that we partake of. Help us find here the light of Christ that will illumine our paths and guide our way. Help us find here your Spirit that will renew our hearts and draw our minds to you. Amen.

PRAYER AFTER COMMUNION: We have gathered in your name, as part of your covenant community. We have come to this covenant because we have seen our Savior's glory. We have celebrated your covenant in word and song and in coming to this table of communion. Help us to be faithful to your covenant now and in the days ahead. Amen.

First Sunday in Lent

Genesis 9:8–17
Psalm 25:1–10
1 Peter 3:18–22
Mark 1:9–15

PRAYER FOR THE BREAD: As we gather at your table again, O God, we remember all you have done for us. You established us as your people, you promised to be our God always, caring for our well-being. You gave us your Son, Jesus Christ, to live and die for us. And you gave us life eternal in Jesus' resurrection. As we eat this bread, help us remember all that it stands for. Let us partake gratefully. Amen.

PRAYER FOR THE CUP: Like the waters of the flood, like the water of our baptism, let your Holy Spirit flow over us, God, as we drink this cup. Help this symbol of the blood of your Son to remind us of the covenant you have had with your people throughout generations. Let us drink, remember, and renew our covenant with you. Amen.

UNIFIED PRAYER: O God, who gives us truth, mercy, and love, let us feel your presence as we gather around your table again this Sunday. Help us remember your covenant long ago with your people. Remind us of that renewed covenant in the ministry of Jesus. Let us accept in thanksgiving the gift of life eternal given to us in the death and resurrection of our Lord Jesus Christ. As we eat this bread and drink from this cup, help us walk your path of steadfast love and faithfulness as a covenant people. Amen.

PRAYER AFTER COMMUNION: Thanks be to God for the everlasting covenant from generation to generation through Jesus Christ our Lord. Amen.

Second Sunday in Lent

Genesis 17:1–7, 15–16
Psalm 22:23–31
Romans 4:13–25
Mark 8:31–38 or *9:2–9*

PRAYER FOR THE BREAD: Throughout the generations, dear God, your steadfast love has sustained us. You have taught us to live by faith. Although we struggle with fears and questions, you still love us and care for us. In breaking this bread, we affirm that we are Christ's disciples, and we acknowledge that Jesus Christ is our savior and your Son. Help us to walk the paths of faith and to be guided by your Spirit. Amen.

PRAYER FOR THE CUP: We will praise you, O God, and tell of your wonderful name. You have not turned away from your people in their need, but have sent Jesus Christ to bring hope and love. As we drink this cup, we remember that your Messiah did not come to lord it over others, but to give his own life that we might live. In this, we have been delivered into your life, O God. Help us to be faithful to you, that your name may be proclaimed to all generations. Amen.

UNIFIED PRAYER: God of the ages, we remember in awe and wonder how you have shown your love to your people. To Abraham and Sarah you gave a promise, and today we are among their spiritual descendants. To the disciples you gave Jesus, and through faith they were able to recognize him as the Messiah. To us you have given the living Christ, who dwells with us today and will be with your people always. As we eat this bread and drink this cup, we remember the Messiah who died for us, and we celebrate the living Christ in our midst. We thank you for moments such as these that help deepen our faith and that help to tie us to your people of all generations. We pray through your Spirit. Amen.

PRAYER AFTER COMMUNION: We praise you, dear God, for being with us today in this Lenten communion service. Help us to be mindful of the physical and spiritual needs of others as you are of ours. Amen.

Third Sunday in Lent

Exodus 20:1–17
Psalm 19
1 Corinthians 1:18–25
John 2:13–22

PRAYER FOR THE BREAD: God, you gave us words by which to live, laws to govern our lives, a Christ to teach us how to live, a Savior to die for us. Yet we do not always follow your ways. The Christian way is difficult and we often fail. As we take this bread, let it strengthen us in our daily lives. Help us keep your commandments as we walk this Lenten way. Amen.

PRAYER FOR THE CUP: Dear God, we remember that Jesus Christ poured out his life-giving blood for us as a way of showing your love for us. Now we, your grateful people, drink from this cup, symbolic of this wonderful love. We pray that through this ritual act, we will grow in fellowship with you and one another. Show us ways that your Spirit can work through us so that we can share life-giving opportunities with others. Amen.

UNIFIED PRAYER: Like the Jews of old, we wait at the foot of the mountain for laws. Like the Jews, we wait for a leader to show us the way. In accepting Jesus as our Lord and Savior, we acknowledge that we know about the Christian life. Yet it seems so hard at times to follow the teachings of Jesus crucified. Yet it is in these words that this meal is made real to us. By eating the bread and drinking from the cup, we begin to know the meaning of the words "Christ crucified"—and your great love for us, God. Help us during this Lenten season to live more fully in your law of love. Amen.

PRAYER AFTER COMMUNION: Loving God, in this Lenten season we are deeply aware of the divine love and human sin that led Jesus Christ to the cross. Here at this table we have reenacted the meal that Christ had with his disciples in the shadow of that cross. Help us to live in response to that love, so that our words and actions may point beyond ourselves to you. Amen.

Fourth Sunday in Lent

Numbers 21:4–9
Psalm 107:1–3, 17–22
Ephesians 2:1–10
John 3:14–21

PRAYER FOR THE BREAD: O great God of mercy, you have given us so much for which to praise you. You have given us life, you have given us many second chances, you have given us forgiveness. Yet the greatest gift you have given us is your Son, Jesus Christ. In believing in Jesus Christ, we are given salvation and eternal life. In grace we take this bread, knowing we could not have earned it. We eat it thankfully, remembering your Son's body given for us. Amen.

PRAYER FOR THE CUP: As we come to this table today, Lord, we ask your forgiveness for the sins we have committed against you and against any of your children. We read your words of grace and forgiveness, and try again to be the children you would want us to be. Send us your Holy Spirit to guide us in all our efforts to be followers of Christ. As we drink from this cup, help it to strengthen us to walk in your path. Amen.

UNIFIED PRAYER: O God of salvation, as we come to this communion table today, we remember what we have heard from your Word today, "For God so loved the world that he gave his only Son, so that everyone who believes in him may not perish but may have eternal life." We can only imagine the depth of this love—that you would give your Son, Jesus Christ, for all your children. The bread and cup are reminders of this great love—your Son's body and blood—given for us.

It is only by grace that we can take, eat, and drink at this table. It is by grace that we are forgiven our sins. And it is by grace that we accept your great salvation. Amen.

PRAYER AFTER COMMUNION: We give you thanks, O God, for you are good. Your steadfast love endures forever. Throughout the ages you have watched over and protected your children and provided for their needs. Today at this table we have received your care as well. For that, we offer you our thanks. Bless us in the days ahead as you have blessed us at this table. Amen.

Fifth Sunday in Lent

Jeremiah 31:31–34
Psalm 51:1–12
Hebrews 5:5–10
John 12:20–33

PRAYER FOR THE BREAD: Thank you, forgiving God, that we can come to you in our sinful ways and ask for forgiveness. We know you cleanse us from our sins and give us forgiveness. This bread that we will eat helps us understand your great love and forgiveness as we realize it is symbolic of the broken body of your Son, Jesus Christ. In his death and resurrection we are granted a new life. In eating the bread let us ask for forgiveness and feel your spirit within us. Amen.

PRAYER FOR THE CUP: We lift this cup of communion before you, loving God, remembering that when Jesus Christ was lifted up on the cross, it was to gather all people to you. What a wondrous Savior, what wondrous love we have received! Through Christ you have given us this community of faith, you have given us hope, you have given us promise. In drinking this cup we offer our thanks. May your Spirit guide us to come closer to you and to draw others closer to you. Amen.

UNIFIED PRAYER: We thank you, God, that you have been faithful for many generations. You offered your covenant to Abraham and to Moses. You offered your covenant to Israel and Judah. Through Jesus Christ you offer a new covenant of your love and faithfulness to all people. In accepting the bread and cup this day, we affirm this covenant. We testify to your love for us, knowing that you gave your Son for us. Grant us the gift of the Holy Spirit, helping us to share this covenant with your people. Amen.

PRAYER AFTER COMMUNION: God of love, we are a people drawn into covenant with you through your saving work in Jesus Christ. At this table we have affirmed that covenant. We bless you and praise you for this opportunity to celebrate your saving power. Amen.

Sixth Sunday in Lent (Palm Sunday)

Isaiah 50:4–9a
Psalm 118:1–2, 19–29
Philippians 2:5–11
Mark 11:1–11 or *John 12:12–16*

PRAYER FOR THE BREAD:
"Into the city I'd follow the children's band,
waving a branch of a palm tree high in my hand;
one of his heralds, yes, I would sing
loudest hosannas, 'Jesus is King!'"*

Today, triumphant God, we follow your Son into the city, full of praises. And yet, as the week goes by, we forget those praises and doubt that Jesus is the Savior. Forgive us the times we do not acknowledge your Son, and betray him. In giving us this bread, the body of the Savior, you have also given us forgiveness. Help us to walk the difficult path that following Christ's way asks of us during this Holy Week and in all our lives. Amen.

PRAYER FOR THE CUP: O God of spirit and truth, center our spirits in yours. On a joyous day of celebration, when your praise is so great that even the stones would cry out, we pray that you would quiet our hearts so that we may perceive Christ's coming, humble and meek, in our midst. As we drink from this cup of communion, let our attention be centered on the cup of suffering and death that he did not refuse, in order that we might drink worthily from the cup of life and joy that you offer us now. Amen.

*William H. Parker, "Tell me the Stories of Jesus."

UNIFIED PRAYER: Wise God, you have so much to teach us. Help us learn to be of the same mind that was in Christ Jesus, who, though he was in the form of God, emptied himself to live among us. Help us to remember how, when he was in human form, he humbled himself and became obedient to the point of death—even death on a cross. On this Palm Sunday, as we eat this bread and drink from this cup, we express our allegiance to Christ and sing our hosannas. May your Spirit create within us teachable spirits, that we may learn to follow on the path where Christ leads. Amen.

PRAYER AFTER COMMUNION: Eternal God, we thank you for calling us to the way of Christ. We thank you for this table, at which we have been fed. We praise you for sending your Son to be our ruler and savior. Amen.

Maundy Thursday

Exodus 12:1–4, 11–14
Psalm 116:1–2, 12–19
1 Corinthians 11:23–26
John 13:1–17, 31b–35

PRAYER FOR THE BREAD: Gracious God, we thank you that you have mandated this holy meal and invited us to be your guests. Thank you for bringing us together with people we know and love. Yet, help us to remember that we are also in communion with brothers and sisters in Christ in all lands, and even in all times and places. But most important, help us to remember that we break bread in communion with you and your disciples. That moment in a quiet, dark upper room happened only once. Yet in a real way it happens every time two or three are gathered in Christ's name. As we break this bread, refresh, renew, and restore us with the Spirit of Christ. Amen.

PRAYER FOR THE CUP: When Christ and his disciples were surrounded by the hate and fear of the authorities of their day, they gathered together for a meal of love. Help us, God of love, to come to this table in the same manner. Let our love for you, our love for one another, and our love for all your children bind us together here. We come to drink of the cup you offer on this holy night, remembering the words of Paul: "The cup of blessing which we bless, is it not a participation in the blood of Christ?" Help us to take these words seriously. Help us to be drawn into the reality of Christ's presence with us, of Christ's willing sacrifice for us. Help us to be true to the everlasting covenant that we reenact at this table. Hear us as we pray in the name of the one who blessed the cup and who blesses our lives, Jesus Christ our Lord. Amen.

UNIFIED PRAYER: We come to this table, dear God, to hear a story, to see a story, to receive a story. Here, on Maundy Thursday, we participate in this story that you tell, this story of love and sacrifice, this story of resurrection and triumph. We recall the people of Israel, saved from bondage in Egypt. We recall the upper room, where Jesus Christ established a new covenant, saving us from the bondage of sin. The bread we now break reminds us that in Christ you took on human form, that your body was given for us. This cup recalls the new covenant given for us. Bless us now as we partake in this story of salvation. Amen.

PRAYER AFTER COMMUNION: We have reaffirmed our covenant with you, holy God, a covenant sealed at our baptism. We thank you that here we have sensed your love for us and for all your children. We thank you for this communion meal, instituted by Jesus Christ, that helps us remember the covenant of love that was made in the upper room. Strengthen us by your Spirit, that we may live out in our daily lives this covenant we have been given.

Easter Sunday

Acts 10:34–43 or *Isaiah 25:6–9*
Psalm 118:1–2, 14–24
1 Corinthians 15:1–11 or *Acts 10:34–43*
John 20:1–18 or *Mark 16:1–8*

PRAYER FOR THE BREAD: Like the women at the tomb, we come to this miraculous day with news almost too good to believe. Christ has risen from the dead! Your great love, O God, is overwhelming. This ordinary piece of bread symbolizes what you have done for each of us in Jesus Christ. The bread of life is ours for the asking. We celebrate the resurrection with the eating of this bread. Alleluia!

PRAYER FOR THE CUP: Let us be joyful witnesses of the resurrection, gathering around this table to celebrate your gift of eternal life. The cup set before us is the symbol of the sacrifice made by Jesus Christ for each of us. In the presence of the Holy Spirit, let us drink from this cup testifying to your salvation. Great God, we thank you. Amen.

UNIFIED PRAYER: O wondrous and glorious God, we come to your table this Resurrection Sunday filled with joy at the good news we have heard. Christ lives!

The bread we share and the cup we drink this day have renewed meaning as we have just experienced in the past week the passion, betrayal, death, and resurrection of your Son. We feel your love for us. Guide those in our church family who have been baptized this day and will share these symbols of your love for the first time. Let your Holy Spirit wash over them as the very waters of their baptism have so recently done. Let their joy experiencing new life in Christ be a renewal for each of us. Amen.

PRAYER AFTER COMMUNION: "God of unending life, as you raised Jesus from the dead, so with this bread and wine, you raise us from death and fill us with your life. Now reveal your transforming power through us: in the face of chaos, in the house where the angel of death stalks, in each valley of dry bones, where every tomb is sealed and all hope ended. Great and living God, may your life shine through us and all the world become an *Alleluia* sung to you. Amen."*

*From *Thankful Praise,* 105.

Second Sunday of Easter

Acts 4:32–35
Psalm 133
1 John 1:1–2:2
John 20:19–31

PRAYER FOR THE BREAD: O God of past, present, and future, we have received the story in scripture of the risen Lord. We accept what has been passed on to us, the good news of your love. We reenact that story at this table and reaffirm the bond of love that unites us. As we break bread, help us to remember Jesus and the disciples breaking bread in the past. Help us to acknowledge the risen Christ here with us as we break bread today. Help us to have trust and hope that your love will always be with us, even to the end of the age. Amen.

PRAYER FOR THE CUP: We call upon your guiding Spirit, O God, because without it we are helpless and confused. The news of resurrection, of new life in Jesus Christ, is almost impossible to comprehend. Like Thomas, we expect that this good news is too good to be true. We are afraid to believe the best, lest we be disappointed. As we receive this cup, help us to realize that we are receiving an invitation to believe, to respond faithfully, to participate in Christ's resurrection glory, to say with our brother Thomas, "My Lord, and my God!" Amen.

UNIFIED PRAYER: How very good and pleasant it is, O God of love, to be drawn together in community, one with another, to partake of this meal together as one family of faith. Here we lay aside our differences and disagreements and recognize the one who weaves us together into one fabric of love, our risen Lord and Savior, Jesus Christ. Here, as we eat bread and drink of the cup, we recognize and affirm the love Christ has for us and the love that we are called to have for one another. Here we pray that your Spirit will work within us and among us to guide us on your paths of love. Amen.

PRAYER AFTER COMMUNION: We thank you, O God of power, that the risen Christ is in this place. We thank you for the privilege of sharing in this communion meal with the one who first shared it with the disciples in the upper room and shares it still in the power of the resurrection. Bless us as we go forth from this place, and keep our hearts filled with the wonder of your love. Amen.

Third Sunday of Easter

Acts 3:12–19
Psalm 4
1 John 3:1–7
Luke 24:36b–48

PRAYER FOR THE BREAD: We break bread to honor the Christ who died for us, O God of never-ending love. And we break bread in the presence of the risen Christ, O God of mystery and surprise. Open our eyes and our hearts to the presence of the risen Christ today at this table and every day in our lives. Open our minds to encounter the mystery that brings life from death, hope from sorrow. Open us to the workings of your Spirit. In the name of the risen Christ we pray. Amen.

PRAYER FOR THE CUP: There is much in this world to bring us anxiety and fear, O gracious God. Yet you call us to trust in you. We know that sometimes we toss and turn, unable to sleep because of our worries, yet you are there with us even in our darkest moments. As we lift this cup, bless it, and drink it, we remember how, in the shadow of the cross, Christ did the same with his disciples. We remember how out of the tragedy of the cross came the triumph of the resurrection. Bless us with your Spirit that we may find the peace that you offer in Jesus Christ. Amen.

UNIFIED PRAYER: What love you have given us, that we should be called children of God! We could never earn or claim such a title, but you have given it to us. In your love we are sanctified, in your purity we are purified. What a mystery it is that we are gathered around your table at the invitation of Jesus Christ! Here we break bread together, here we drink from the cup together because we are yours. Bless us as we bless the bread, pour your love upon us as we drink the cup. By the work of your Spirit, help us truly to live into the title that you have given us, that the world may know that we are your children. Amen.

PRAYER AFTER COMMUNION: In the holy quiet of this communion service we have once again told Christ's story of suffering and triumph. We have once again acted out the story that shapes our lives. Help us, O God of redeeming love, to let this story's truth transform our lives. By your Spirit's power and in our Savior's name we pray. Amen.

Fourth Sunday of Easter

Acts 4:5–12
Psalm 23
1 John 3:16–24
John 10:11–18

PRAYER FOR THE BREAD: Abide with us, O God of love, as we gather around your table. The bread we break helps us remember our shepherd and guide, Jesus Christ, who helped us pass from death to life. When we remember Christ's body broken for us, we remember that his love was not just in words, but in truth and action. Help us to love others around us, especially those who are poor and in need, as Christ loved us, in truth and action. We thank you for the gift of your Spirit, who gives us the power to believe and to serve. Amen.

PRAYER FOR THE CUP: O God of mercy, help us to remember how Jesus Christ, like a good shepherd, laid down his life for us. We remember as we pour this cup how his life was poured out for us. Yet we know that in this act of sacrifice a new covenant was offered, a covenant of life and hope. The Christ who poured out his life for us is alive today and still leads us in the paths of righteousness. We pray that your Spirit might help us follow in our shepherd's footsteps. Amen.

UNIFIED PRAYER: Good Shepherd, we come at your call. You are the one who, through Jesus Christ, guides us, protects us, and cares for us. You lead us beside the still waters of peace and hope. You provide our daily needs. We thank you for this table spread before us, for the bread and the wine that you have provided, and for the needs of the spirit that they fulfill. We partake of these elements in gratitude and trust, accepting them as a rich sign of your goodness and mercy. Help us to recognize the guiding presence of your Spirit in these moments of communion and in all our days. Amen.

PRAYER AFTER COMMUNION: You have given us this meal by your gracious hand, O Provider God. In it we have been fed and nourished. Help the peace of this moment to transform our lives, that we might faithfully follow you. Amen.

Fifth Sunday of Easter

Acts 8:26–40
Psalm 22:25–31
1 John 4:7–21
John 15:1–8

PRAYER FOR THE BREAD: Author of all love, we gather to share this bread as part of your loving community. In offering this bread up to you, in blessing and breaking it, taking and eating it, we are imitating your Son and our Savior, Jesus Christ. Help us learn how to imitate Christ in other ways. Help us to be more Christlike in the quality of our love and the depth of our compassion, so that all people will know that we are Christ's disciples. Amen.

PRAYER FOR THE CUP: God of all wisdom and power, we are nothing without you, but in you we can be so much. Jesus Christ is the vine, and we are the branches. As we drink this wine, the product of the vine, help us remember the true vine, Jesus Christ. Let his love flow within us and extend through us, that we might bear the fruit of the Christian life. Amen.

UNIFIED PRAYER: We abide in you, O loving God. In you are our strength and substance, our dreams and our visions. We gather around this table to recall that you also abide in us. As we learn to love, learn to hope, and learn to pray, you are there with us and for us. As we break the bread and pour the cup, you are there with us and for us. Through your Spirit's power, help us learn to trust your love, help us learn to reach out to the poor and needy as you have reached out to us. Amen.

PRAYER AFTER COMMUNION: As we go our separate ways, O God, let this time of communion be a reminder that through Jesus Christ you are with us always. Help the love of Christ that we have experienced here shine in us and act through us. Amen.

Sixth Sunday of Easter

Acts 10:44–48
Psalm 98
1 John 5:1–6
John 15:9–17

PRAYER FOR THE BREAD: God of love, we remember as we gather here the love that Jesus Christ has for us. No one has greater love than this, to lay down one's life for one's friends. Jesus Christ called us friends and laid down his life for us. As we break this bread, we remember that Christ gave his body for the sake of our lives. We also remember that as Christ has loved us, so he called us to love one another. May your Spirit help us to grow in that love.

PRAYER FOR THE CUP: The new song we sing as we come to your table is a song of love, O Creator of joy. It is a song of your love, revealed in the life, death, and resurrection of Jesus Christ. We sing of the new covenant established in the upper room the night before our Savior's death, the covenant that binds us to your love. When we drink this cup, we affirm the love that was poured out for us in the upper room, on the cross, and at the open tomb. Our spirits soar at this wondrous love, and we feel the touch of your Spirit in our lives. To you we give our thanks, our love, our all. Amen.

UNIFIED PRAYER: How awesome it is, gracious God, that you have called us as disciples, that you have chosen us to follow the way of love, that you have invited us to this table. The abundance of your grace astonishes us. We come with joy to this place, singing your praises. The bread that we bless, the cup we raise, tell the story of your love revealed to us in Jesus Christ. As we eat and drink, help us to treasure what we have been given. Let the love we celebrate here transform our lives to your purposes. By the power of your Spirit and in the name of Christ our Savior we pray. Amen.

PRAYER AFTER COMMUNION: God, you have done marvelous things, and you deserve our praise. We have received the gift of your presence in this time of communion, and your Spirit has opened our hearts to the outpouring of your love. Keep our hearts open in the days ahead so that when we have the opportunity to love others, we will recognize in it the opportunity to love you. Amen.

Seventh Sunday of Easter

Acts 1:15–17, 21–26
Psalm 1
1 John 5:9–13
John 17:6–19

PRAYER FOR THE BREAD: We thank you, God, for eternal life in Jesus Christ. When we eat this bread, symbolizing the body of your Son, we are reminded of your great love for us. In these weeks following Easter Sunday, it is easy to remember the resurrection; help us throughout the rest of the year to be "Easter People"—a people testifying to your great power. Let this bread give us the strength to be that witness. Amen.

PRAYER FOR THE CUP: As Jesus prayed for his disciples' safety in a time of trial, we pray also for safety and guidance in our lives. This cup from which we drink represents a commitment of Jesus' life in a time of trial. In drinking from this cup, we know that Jesus died for us. Let us come, as one people, praising your name for this gift of life. Then let us go from the table with the Holy Spirit's guidance for our lives.

UNIFIED PRAYER:

> If you will trust in God to guide you,
> and hope in God through all your ways,
> God will give strength, what-e'er betide you,
> and bear you through all the evil days.
> Who trusts in God's unchanging love
> builds on the rock that will not move.*

God, we thank for your laws and the teachings of Jesus to guide us in the ways of discipleship. Most of all, we thank you for your Son, Jesus Christ, who died that we will have life. We remember the body and blood of Christ Jesus as we eat the bread and drink from the cup.

> Sing, pray, and keep God's ways unswerving;
> so do your own part faithfully,
> and trust God's word; though undeserving,
> you'll find God's promise true to be.
> God never will forsake in need,
> the soul that trusts in God indeed.*

PRAYER OF COMMUNION: We have been to your open table, O God of new life, and we have been to the open tomb. May these moments of communion that we have just experienced lead us into a process of receiving an open mind to your word and an open heart to your love. Amen.

*Georg Neumark, "If You Will Trust in God to Guide You."

Day of Pentecost

Ezekiel 37:1–14 or *Acts 2:1–21*
Psalm 104:24–34, 35b
Romans 8:22–27
John 15:26–27; 16:4b–15

PRAYER FOR THE BREAD: On this day of Pentecost, we come to you, O life-giving God. We gather to eat the bread that represents Christ's body given for us, the bread that represents Christ's life. We gather to receive the Spirit that Christ promised, the Spirit that brings us new life. Thank you for these gifts: the gift of life, the gift of bread, the gift of your Spirit. As you have offered these gifts to us, so we offer our lives to you. Transform our lives that others might see your love working in us and through us. We pray in Christ's name and spirit. Amen.

PRAYER FOR THE CUP: Where there is death, O living God, your Spirit brings life. Grant us new life in your Spirit as we gather to drink this cup. In so doing, we remember your life poured out for us in Jesus Christ's death on the cross. Help us remember your Spirit poured out on the church, as well, a Spirit that brings newness and hope. Let your Spirit work in our midst, giving us the guidance we need to be your servants. In Jesus' name we pray. Amen.

UNIFIED PRAYER:

O gracious God,
You have given us bread as
your Son's body.
We have taken the bread in
remembrance.
You give us wine as your son's, our Lord
Jesus Christ's, blood.
We drink in humility as we
realize your great love for us.
You have given us the Holy Spirit
to be with us always. We receive
the Spirit in grace and thanksgiving.
As we eat the bread,
share the wine,
and receive the gift of the Holy Spirit,
direct our lives to always
reflect your love.
Help us share this great
gift with all your people.

PRAYER AFTER COMMUNION: Gracious Spirit, dwell with us. Help these moments of communion that we have just observed to fill us with the Spirit of Christ, so that we may carry your blessing into the world. Amen.

Trinity Sunday (First Sunday after Pentecost)

Isaiah 6:1–8
Psalm 29
Romans 8:12–17
John 3:1–17

PRAYER FOR THE BREAD: God, there is no earthly way we can comprehend your love for us. You not only gave us life on earth, but you gave us your Son, Jesus Christ, to die for us that we might have life eternally with you. In your great love, you sacrificed your only Son. The broken bread that we share together reminds us of that sacrifice. We eat the bread in thanksgiving for your great love. Amen.

PRAYER FOR THE CUP: O God, you are so powerful that your voice is heard over all creation. Yet you are a tender God, loving the people whom you created. We pray as we drink from this cup, reminding us that you gave your only Son that we might have life always with you, that we will be empowered by the Holy Spirit to show your love in our lives. Amen.

UNIFIED PRAYER: O great and powerful God, whose powerful voice is heard in thunder and fire, yet whose tender love gave us his Son, we come to this table as your children. Guide us to lead spirit-filled lives so that we may truly show that we are your heirs. As we take the bread and cup this day, help us to realize the meaning of your wonderful love for us, that you gave your only Son, whom we honor in this holy meal. Send your Spirit to call us into life with you. Amen.

PRAYER AFTER COMMUNION: We have eaten the bread and drunk from the cup knowing we are heirs of your great and profound love. In Jesus Christ we glory! Amen.

*Proper 4**
Sunday between May 29 and June 4

(if after Trinity Sunday)
1 Samuel 3:1–10 (11–20)
Psalm 139:1–6, 13–18
2 Corinthians 4:5–12
Mark 2:23–3:6

PRAYER FOR THE BREAD: Wonderful are your works, O Lord! You have made each of us, you know our wants and needs. You know when we are discouraged, perplexed. Yet because of your great works, we know we carry the spirit of the risen Christ within us, giving us the strength to overcome all earthly trials. Within us we have a treasure in you, O Lord. As we eat this bread, call us to draw strength from the power of your love in Jesus Christ. Amen.

PRAYER FOR THE CUP: You have searched us, O God, and you know us even better than we know ourselves. Although we can hide much from others, although we can hide much from ourselves, we can hide nothing from you. You see us for who we are and still you love us, in spite of every sin, failing, and weakness. This cup from which we drink is a reminder of your love, manifested in our Lord Jesus Christ. As we drink from it, help us to realize how close you are to us, and help us to realize how close you are calling us to be to you. Help us to be sensitive to the presence of your Spirit in our midst, in these moments and in every day. Amen.

*For Propers 1–3, see pp. 30–35.

UNIFIED PRAYER: God, who calls each of us to be your servants, help us to listen well to your voice. As we hear your call to belief, help us to practice in a world that often, even among believers, has no depth and no outward appearances of belief. Reveal your call in the plight of the poor, the hungry, the destitute, those whose humanity is not recognized because of physical characteristics, and those who suffer because of the treatment they receive from "God-fearing" people.

In the taking of this bread and cup, strengthen our call to the ministry of Jesus Christ, in whose name we celebrate at this table. And as we eat, let us renew our calling so that we might say, "Speak, Yahweh, your servant listens."*

PRAYER AFTER COMMUNION: In our darkness, your light has shone. In our foolishness, we have received knowledge of your love and will. In our frailty we have received strength. Thank you, O God, for these moments of communion in which we feel your presence and receive your gifts. Let your Spirit work in this congregation that it might truly witness to your love. Amen.

*Adapted from Megan McKenna, *Keepers of the Story* (Maryknoll, N.Y.: Orbis Press, 1997), 56.

Proper 5
Sunday between June 5 and June 11

1 Samuel 8:4–11 (12–15), 16–20 (11:14–15)
Psalm 138
2 Corinthians 4:13–5:1
Mark 3:20–35

PRAYER FOR THE BREAD: God, we come together this morning to break bread in thanksgiving for your steadfast love, which endures forever. Each of us has brought to this table our joys, hurts, successes, and failures. In all of these, we sense your presence, especially as visibly shown in the bread, the body of Jesus Christ. Bless us as we take this bread and bless it and eat together, as Christ taught us. Let us fully realize your love and care for each of us. Amen.

PRAYER FOR THE CUP: God of all creation, you have called us to love you and serve you. Your word of love and salvation has been planted in our hearts as we have accepted Christ as our Savior. Help this time of communion to be a time when that word can grow and take fruit. We ask you to bless this cup, that in drinking from it we may remember Christ's self-giving love. Let the spiritual nourishment that we find here strengthen us so that we may practice that love in a troubled world. Amen.

UNIFIED PRAYER: Dear God, we give you thanks with all our hearts. When we are in troubled times, you preserve us and deliver us. When we are weak, you give us strength. When we are troubled, you give us peace. When our lives and health are threatened, you give us hope. This feast of communion that we now celebrate is a sign of your steadfast love and presence. Bless the bread that we break, that we might remember that Christ gave himself for us. Bless the cup that we pour, that we might remember Christ's self-giving love poured out for us. As we reflect upon Christ's love for us, we pray that your Spirit will help us grow in our love for Christ and for one another. Amen.

PRAYER AFTER COMMUNION: Everlasting and ever-caring God, these moments of communion may end, but your steadfast love endures forever. Help us to be aware of this love throughout our lives. Help us to be living witnesses to your love, that in the ways we give, the ways we care, the ways we love, others may see Christ's presence. Amen.

Proper 6
Sunday between June 12 and June 18

> *1 Samuel 15:34–16:13*
> *Psalm 20*
> *2 Corinthians 5:6–17 (11–13)*
> *Mark 4:26–34*

PRAYER FOR THE BREAD: From wheat seed scattered on the ground comes the grain of which this bread is made. From hearing your word, following Christ's teachings, and walking by faith, we grow as Christians. We confess that many times we act immaturely as your children. As we take this bread, the body of your Son, Jesus Christ, forgive us and help us grow to new life in Christ. Amen.

PRAYER FOR THE CUP: Thank you, God, for the opportunity to come to this table, to bless this cup in communion together with your Spirit. It is so easy to think of ourselves and others in human terms, to forget that in Christ we are new creations. Transform our attitudes as we drink this cup, that we may act in bold, loving, and creative ways to proclaim your gospel in word and deed. Amen.

UNIFIED PRAYER: O God of mystery, you choose a king from the youngest of the sons, you tell us that faith the size of a mustard seed, so tiny, will increase greatly. You tell us to walk by faith, not by sight. You are full of surprises. This bread, the staple of each meal, the grapes made into common, everyday wine are the blood and body of your Son, Jesus Christ, who died for us all. Let us eat and drink and seek to understand your ways in our lives. Amen.

PRAYER AFTER COMMUNION: "Help us remember that at every meal God and all God's family are our companions, and that God nourishes us so that we may feed the world."* Go, nourished, and seek to serve. Amen.

*Pamela Moeller, *Exploring Worship Anew* (St. Louis: Chalice Press, 1998), 39.

Proper 7
Sunday between June 19 and June 25

1 Samuel 17:(1a, 4–11, 19–23), 32–49
Psalm 9:9–20
2 Corinthians 6:1–13
Mark 4:35–41

PRAYER FOR THE BREAD: We sing your praises, God of power, and we proclaim your saving deeds. In Jesus Christ you have brought deliverance to your people. We come now to the communion table, remembering that Jesus offered his life that we might know your love. May the bread that we break now help us to remember Christ's body. As we eat this bread, may it also remind us that we are part of Christ's body today and that we are called to heal and help, to set free the oppressed, to serve, and to love. Send your Spirit into our lives so that we may truly be Christ's people. Amen.

PRAYER FOR THE CUP: Sometimes, dear God, our lives seem out of control and we are frightened, as if we were on a storm-tossed sea. Then we hear Christ's words, "Peace, be still." Let these moments of communion be a time of peace, a time of stillness, so that we may orient our lives around your love and purpose for us. We now ask you to bless the cup, and bless us as we drink from it, to live in your peace. May your Spirit touch our spirits with your presence. Amen.

UNIFIED PRAYER: To you we sing our praise, O God of deliverance. Through Jesus Christ you have called us, saved us, and named us. You have calmed the stormy seas of our lives. You have set aside this time of communion that we now observe and made it holy. Through this time the rest of our days have meaning and purpose. This bread we eat and this cup we drink bind us together in harmony with you and recall to us how Jesus Christ helped us find freedom and wholeness. Let us experience your blessing as we share these elements. Grant us the peace of your Spirit. In the name of Christ we pray. Amen.

PRAYER AFTER COMMUNION: We have come to this table, dear God, to remember Jesus Christ and to let Christ work within us and among us. Through Christ's Spirit, may our daily lives be expressions of your love. Amen.

Proper 8
Sunday between June 26 and July 2

2 Samuel 1:1, 17–27
Psalm 130
2 Corinthians 8:7–15
Mark 5:21–43

PRAYER FOR THE BREAD: This day, O Lord, we come to your table in an attitude of prayer. We offer thanks that we can pray to you when we are in sorrow or in joy. We can pray, asking forgiveness or giving praise to you. You hear our every word, and we feel your presence.

Now at this communion table, we feel your presence in the breaking of bread, which represents your Son's body. We offer prayers of thanksgiving for your great love for us. Amen.

PRAYER FOR THE CUP: We are bound to you, God, in hope and in your steadfast love. In the death and resurrection of your Son Jesus Christ, we are truly aware of your steadfast love for each of us. This cup before us reminds of this great redeeming power. Let us drink and praise your name! Amen.

UNIFIED PRAYER:
My faith looks up to thee,
thou Lamb of Calvary,
Savior divine!
Now hear me while I pray;
take all my guilt away;
oh, let me from this day
be wholly thine.*

In faith we come to this holy table knowing we can come to you in prayer for whatever our needs may be. We know your forgiveness, your healing. We know you hear our prayers of sorrow and despair. We pray in faith, knowing you will answer us. Our taking of this bread and cup is the result of our faith knowing your Son, Jesus Christ, died for us. And in eating and drinking these symbols, we lift our voices in prayers of praise and thanksgiving, knowing we are wholly yours. Amen.

PRAYER AFTER COMMUNION: We have gathered at your table, dear God, at your invitation. Here we have found refreshment and joy, forgiveness and love. Now we hear your invitation to go out into the world and witness to your love, in our words and in our deeds. Grant that through your Spirit we may have the faith and love to accept that invitation, as well. Amen.

*Ray Palmer, "My Faith Looks Up to Thee."

Proper 9
Sunday between July 3 and July 9

2 Samuel 5:1–5, 9–10
Psalm 48
2 Corinthians 12:2–10
Mark 6:1–13

PRAYER FOR THE BREAD: You are great, O God, and greatly to be praised. Your steadfast love endures forever. As we gather around this table to break bread, we remember how Jesus healed and preached, and how he released people from their torment, to let them know your good news. As we accept this bread to eat, let us accept the presence of the living Christ in our hearts. Help us by your Spirit's power to be faithful to you as you are faithful to us. Amen.

PRAYER FOR THE CUP: God of peace, God of hope, we come to the table that you have set. We come to drink from the cup that Jesus Christ gave to us, the cup of the new covenant. Bless us as we drink this cup and pledge ourselves to the way of Christ. Amen.

UNIFIED PRAYER: Your name, O God, is great and reaches to the ends of the earth. Yet we know that you tenderly care for us as individuals. We know that you are with us in all our life struggles. This bread and this cup remind us that you have called us, that you do care for us, for they remind us of Jesus Christ. As we eat and drink, help us to renew our commitment to serve and follow you. Watch over us in your Spirit. Amen.

PRAYER AFTER COMMUNION: Thank you, dear God, for the story of love and salvation that is ours through Jesus Christ. Thank you for the elements that we have shared, the bread and the wine that touch our lives so deeply. Help us walk in your way, through Jesus Christ our Lord. Amen.

Proper 10
Sunday between July 10 and 16

2 Samuel 6:1–5, 12b–19
Psalm 24
Ephesians 1:3–14
Mark 6:14–29

PRAYER FOR THE BREAD: We come with joy to this table, gracious God, for we have heard your invitation. You have chosen us in Christ to be your family. We stand in awe at the beauty and power of your word, at the generosity of your self-giving love. In your wisdom and love, you have given us the living bread of Christ Jesus, the bread that gives eternal life. As we eat this physical bread this morning, help us realize that Jesus Christ is our true bread, our true source of life. Guide us in your Spirit. Amen.

PRAYER FOR THE CUP: God of everlasting love, you have called us to be your children. You have poured out your grace upon us. You have forgiven us and redeemed us through the blood of Jesus Christ. Although we may never totally understand the mystery of your will, we do know that your love for us is deep and rich. Now we gather to drink this cup and to remember the source of our redemption. Help us as we drink to realize that this is a sign of your redemption and the inheritance of love that we receive as your children. Touch us with your Spirit that we may praise your glorious name. Amen.

UNIFIED PRAYER: We come to this table, God of might and power, with humble hearts. As we see the beauty of your created world, as we marvel at the joy of being alive, we are filled with awe and wonder. Although we struggle with our own lack of faith and trust, we know deep within us that you are God, and we seek to follow your way. Help us to learn from Jesus Christ the paths of love, witness, and service. The bread that we eat and the cup that we bless are precious reminders of the one we are called to follow. Come into our hearts as we partake, and fill us with your love. Bless us by your Spirit so that we may be sources of joy and inspiration to others. Amen.

PRAYER AFTER COMMUNION: We, your children, have come before you in love and joy. We have found the strength and wisdom of your Spirit at this table. Guide us by your Spirit, O God, as we go forth from this place, that we may truly live as your children. Amen.

Proper 11
Sunday between July 17 and 23

2 Samuel 7:1–14a
Psalm 89:20–37
Ephesians 2:11–22
Mark 6:30–34, 53–56

PRAYER FOR THE BREAD: As Christ fed the multitudes in the wilderness, we ask you to feed us now, O God. Although we are well-fed, we are a hungry people spiritually. We need more than what this world offers. We are like sheep without a shepherd. Bless this bread as Christ blessed the loaves and fishes in Galilee and as he blessed the bread in the upper room. Let your Spirit fill us, let your love be multiplied in our hearts, in our lives, and in our church. Amen.

PRAYER FOR THE CUP: We come to you, Holy One, knowing that you are a God of faithfulness, a God of steadfast love. We praise you for the covenants that you have made with your people through the millennia of history. We especially thank you for the covenant made in Jesus Christ, that the world might know your salvation. The cup we share now calls us to remember that we are part of that covenant, sealed in the upper room. Bless us by your Spirit as we partake. Amen.

UNIFIED PRAYER: Once we were without Christ; now we are in Christ. Once we were divided and alienated; now we are one. You are the God who breaks down the walls of separation, who draws your people together in peace. You have reconciled us at the cross of Christ, and we are no longer strangers. We have been welcomed into the household of God. This communion meal that we now share is a sign that, through Jesus Christ, we are members of your family. As we partake of these elements, help us to live in peace. Guide us through your Spirit so that we may be peacemakers. Amen.

PRAYER AFTER COMMUNION: We are part of your dwelling place, O God of peace. We are part of your holy temple. We have shared in the meal that Jesus Christ, our cornerstone, instituted for us. As we go forth from this place, we pray that others will be able to see your peace and love in our lives. Amen.

Proper 12
Sunday between July 24 and 30

2 Samuel 11:1–15
Psalm 14
Ephesians 3:14–21
John 6:1–21

PRAYER FOR THE BREAD: Help us, O God, to love you as you have first loved us. Help us to realize that if we are to love you, we are to love one another as well. Give us a spirit of sharing, so that we may offer you what we have. Help us to realize that we break the bread in order to share it, so that we might act out the message of Christ and his self-sacrificing love. Challenge our spirits so that we may respond to a hungry world with caring and generosity. As we eat this bread of communion, may we be empowered by your Spirit to share what we have in order that it may be multiplied by your love. Hear us as we pray in Jesus' name. Amen.

PRAYER FOR THE CUP: O God of power and abundance, the love you have for us in Jesus Christ surpasses all our hopes and expectations. We aren't able to even comprehend the breadth and length and height and depth of that love. Yet, as we raise this cup and drink from it, we realize that we are nourished and strengthened by that love. In this moment of communion, we realize that the Christ who shared a cup in the upper room is the Christ who lives in our hearts. Bless us as we drink this cup, and strengthen us through the power of your Spirit. Amen.

UNIFIED PRAYER: God of generosity and power, we come before you hungry and full of need. We have so little to offer, yet we know that you have the power to transform what we give and make out of it something wonderful. We offer pieces of bread and cups of wine. Take what we offer, and give us the presence of the living Christ. Nourish our souls and refresh our spirits today as Jesus Christ fed the crowd by the Sea of Galilee. Through your Spirit, grant that we may encounter here the wondrous love of Jesus Christ, our Lord and Savior. Amen.

PRAYER AFTER COMMUNION: As generations of believers have done since Christ gathered his disciples in the upper room, we have come to your table, gracious God. The power of your Spirit has worked within us and among us, as it will in all generations. To you be glory forever. Amen.

Proper 13
Sunday between July 31 and August 6

2 Samuel 11:26—12:13a
Psalm 51:1—12
Ephesians 4:1—16
John 6:24—35

PRAYER FOR THE BREAD: We come to this table, O God, our gracious host, because we love your holy name. As in Jesus Christ you fed the multitudes with bread, so we come to you—hungry for the bread of inner peace, of strength and hope. Bless us we eat this bread of communion and are fed by your grace. We pray for your Spirit's gifts, so that we may live the kind of lives to which we have been called: lives of gentleness, patience, love, and service, as befits followers of Jesus Christ. Amen.

PRAYER FOR THE CUP: Faithful and forgiving God, you catch us and lift us up when we fall. When our spirits are low, your Spirit gives us encouragement. When we hunger for your presence, you fill our needs. When we sin and stray from your paths, you call us to repentance and offer us forgiveness. The cup we raise today recalls our Savior's last earthly meal, and the supreme love that was revealed then. As we share this cup, let us share the inexpressible love and the indescribable peace that your Spirit offers. Amen.

UNIFIED PRAYER: There are many forces, without and within, that divide and fragment us, dear God. Pride and fear, prejudice and hatred separate us from our brothers and sisters in Christ. Although we may rationalize our separations, we know deep within that you want us to be one, that you want us to be at peace. Let us be one, let us be yours, as we eat this bread. Let us be one, let us be yours, as we drink this cup. Help us to work, witness, and live as one, bound by the unity of your Spirit. Amen.

PRAYER AFTER COMMUNION: It is not the ritual that we have done here that brings you pleasure, O God. It is, rather, what happened in our hearts and spirits as the ritual occurred. As we conclude this time of communion, we offer these hearts and spirits to you in love and obedience. We pray that your work of forgiveness and transformation may continue in our hearts as we go from this table. Amen.

Proper 14
Sunday between August 7 and 13

2 Samuel 18:5–9, 15, 31–33
Psalm 130
Ephesians 4:25–5:2
John 6:35, 41–51

PRAYER FOR THE BREAD: We are here, gracious God, because you have invited us. We are here to eat bread and to affirm that Jesus Christ is the bread of the world. In Christ we receive new life, and the power to live by your grace and your Spirit. Bless us, dear God, as we partake. Amen.

PRAYER FOR THE CUP: God of peace, we thank you for this community of faith and for your church everywhere. It is here that we learn the ways of Christ that we may live the paths of peace in a troubled world. Help us to learn at your table how to be kind and tenderhearted, as through Jesus Christ we have received your kindness and compassion. As we drink this cup, we remember how Christ loved us so much that he gave himself as an offering. Bless us in your Spirit, that the love we have received from you may be the love we express to the world. Amen.

UNIFIED PRAYER: In you, O God, we find our hope. In you we find steadfast love. In you we find redemption, through Jesus Christ. In this meal we remember that hope, that love, and that redemption as we reflect on Christ's saving work for us. In taking the bread and the cup we recall Christ, the living bread, eating and drinking with the disciples in the upper room. We affirm in faith Christ's presence here with us, and we affirm our hope that in Christ we will never be separated from your love. Be with us and bless us with your Spirit. Amen.

PRAYER AFTER COMMUNION: We leave this holy place now, dear God, to share the love that we have experienced here with the world around us. We are grateful that as you were with us here, you will be with us there. Let us be able to see your presence in the faces and places of daily life as we have experienced your presence here. Amen.

Proper 15
Sunday between August 14 and 20

1 Kings 2:10–12; 3:3–14
Psalm 111
Ephesians 5:15–20
John 6:51–58

PRAYER FOR THE BREAD: Gracious God, how grateful we are that you give your children bread. Each day you provide for our needs. Just as the spiritually starved of Jesus' day heard him say, "I am the bread of life," so we too receive the spiritual food of Christ's presence. We come to be nourished, strengthened, and encouraged by the breaking of bread. Help us to share with the world the bread of life that is Jesus Christ, that others might be fed as we are today. Lead us by your Spirit. Amen.

PRAYER FOR THE CUP: What a joyous thing it is, O God, that we can sing your praises. What a wonderful gift you have given us in Jesus Christ, our Lord and Savior. We praise your great works and wonderful deeds, all your acts of loving-kindness and compassion. The cup we drink at this table of communion is an emblem of your self-giving nature. It reminds us of who we are and of whose we are. As we drink from it, let us be led by your Spirit to commit ourselves to your way. Amen.

UNIFIED PRAYER: Holy and awesome is your name, O God, for you have sent us redemption and you have given us an everlasting covenant. Often we are tempted to act in foolish, selfish, and hateful ways, and not to seek the wisdom of love that you offer your children. Yet you care for us and offer the food of your presence to us, as we see in this communion meal today. As we eat and drink here today, we pray that you would grant us hearts of wisdom, that we may discern your will and your ways. Help us find in your Spirit the wisdom and strength that we need to act as your loving children. Amen.

PRAYER AFTER COMMUNION: We are your people; you are our God. Help us to be a faithful and loving people, as you are a faithful and loving God. As we leave this table, let your ways of peace and love be seen in our faces, our hearts, and our actions. Amen.

Proper 16
Sunday between August 21 and 27

1 Kings 8:(1, 6, 10–11), 22–30, 41–43
Psalm 84
Ephesians 6:10–20
John 6:56–69

PRAYER FOR THE BREAD: God, who supplies our every need, we come in thanksgiving this day for the bread that is on the table before us. By faith we affirm that this is the bread of heaven that will "feed us, 'till we want no more." This is the bread that will satisfy our spiritual hunger. This is the bread, the body of Jesus Christ. Bless us as we eat, help us find strength in your Spirit. Amen.

PRAYER FOR THE CUP: In you, dear God, we find our strength; in worshiping you we find our joy. Your love shines upon us as light shines from the sun. You give us the gifts of memory and hope that help us find you in our present. In drinking this cup at your table, we remember Christ and the disciples in the upper room, we proclaim our hope in the Christ who is to come, and we affirm the Christ who is in our midst. May that Christ be in our hearts and minds at this table and forever. Amen.

UNIFIED PRAYER: Wonderful God, you are everywhere! Heaven and earth cannot contain you, let alone this church where we worship. Yet we do have your promise that you are here in our midst. As Christ promised his disciples, he is here and you are here when we gather in Christ's name. We stand on that promise in this service of communion, and we ask your blessing upon this bread and this cup. May your Spirit help this congregation discern your presence here, and may it help us discern your presence in the daily world as well. Amen.

PRAYER AFTER COMMUNION: Here at your table, O God, we have come seeking faith, love, strength, and wisdom to help us live as your faithful servants. We thank you for the opportunity to commune with you and pray that our hearts will be open to accept the gifts that we came to seek. Amen.

Proper 17
Sunday between August 28 and September 3

Song of Songs 2:8–13
Psalm 45:1–2, 6–9
James 1:17–27
Mark 7:1–8, 14–15, 21–23

PRAYER FOR THE BREAD: We come to this table, O God, not because we are pure or holy, but because you have invited us as we are. Our lives are fragmented and confused, yet your love for us is unfailing. The bread of communion that we now share is a reminder of Christ's body, given for us. Use this moment to let your Spirit work within us and among us to bring us your peace. In Christ's name we pray. Amen.

PRAYER FOR THE CUP: God of love and power, as we lift this cup of communion before you, draw us out of our self-centered ways. Help us reflect upon the love of Jesus Christ poured out for us on the cross. Transform us through your Spirit, so that our hearts may overflow with your praise. Transform us through your Spirit that our actions of love and compassion to those in need may be consistent with the love and compassion that you have shown us. Amen.

UNIFIED PRAYER: Every perfect gift comes from you, eternal God. In you, there is no shadow of turning. Your compassion never fails. Help us learn at this table how you sent Christ to be our living bread and how you poured yourself out for us in Christ's sacrifice on the cross. As we eat this bread and drink this cup, we celebrate your faithfulness and compassion. Through the presence of your Spirit, help us learn to be faithful to you and compassionate to others. Amen.

PRAYER AFTER COMMUNION: God of all goodness, at this table you have given us the resources of the Spirit that we need to live as your children. When times of struggle come, help us to use these resources of goodness, peace, and faith. As prayer has brought us close to you here at this table, help us to realize that we can always come close to you in prayer, no matter where we are. Amen.

Proper 18
Sunday between September 4 and 10

Proverbs 22:1–2, 8–9, 22–23
Psalm 125
James 2:1–10 (11–13), 14–17
Mark 7:24–37

PRAYER FOR THE BREAD: God of justice and love, you have made this table for all your children. Sometimes we would limit others' access to it by our attitudes of superiority. Help us to realize that before you we are all spiritually needy. The bread we take, break, and bless reminds us of the love that Jesus Christ had for us and for all our brothers and sisters. In eating this bread we remember that we are called to love others as we love ourselves. Let your Spirit lead us on the paths of love. Amen.

PRAYER FOR THE CUP: O God, all too often we put our trust in that which does not last, that which is not ultimately secure. We pray at this communion table that we will learn to trust you with all our hearts. We pray that we may realize that your love surrounds us and supports us. Help us to remember as we drink this cup that Jesus Christ trusted you completely, even in the shadow of the cross. Let your Spirit teach us to trust enough to love you and to love others. Amen.

UNIFIED PRAYER: Creator God, you have made us all. As we come to this table, help us to recognize and to put aside the false distinctions that divide us from one another—distinctions of wealth, of status, of race, of gender, of education, of nationality. Help us to realize that at this table we are all one, created by one God, servants of one Christ. Let us eat the bread and drink from the cup in humility and love, as Christ has taught us. Guide us by your Spirit on the paths of justice, fairness, and peace. Amen.

PRAYER AFTER COMMUNION: We have come to this table, O God, because we are poor and needy in things of the Spirit. Here we have found refreshment and strength. As we leave, help us to share with others the love that we have found in you. Amen.

Proper 19
Sunday between September 11 and 17

Proverbs 1:20–33
Psalm 19
James 3:1–12
Mark 8:27–38

PRAYER FOR THE BREAD: As we come to this holy table, let the words of our mouths and the meditations of our hearts be acceptable, O Lord. By this act of taking bread, we proclaim your son as Messiah. Let the words we speak in our everyday lives show our commitment to be your followers. Amen.

PRAYER FOR THE CUP: This cup that is before us represents the total commitment of your Son, Jesus Christ—the commitment to give his life for us. By the drinking from this cup, we show our desire to take up the cross and follow Jesus. Help us to listen to your word and follow your path. Amen.

UNIFIED PRAYER: There is nothing great and wonderful that you did not create, O God. The world and all that is in it, your laws and commandments show us your glory. In the name of Jesus Christ, the Messiah, we gather at this table, proclaiming your greatest work—the resurrection. As we eat this bread and drink from this cup, we are recipients of your great and saving works. In thanksgiving we honor your name. Amen.

PRAYER AFTER COMMUNION: We thank you, dear God, for the opportunity to share at Christ's table. Help these moments of community with you and with our fellow believers to give us guidance and strength that we may live as your witnesses. Amen.

Proper 20
Sunday between September 18 and 24

Proverbs 31:10–31
Psalm 1
James 3:13–4:3, 7–8a
Mark 9:30–37

PRAYER FOR THE BREAD: We pray, O giver of wisdom, that you will help us discern what is right and pleasing to you. We know that true wisdom comes only from you. Help us to be filled with righteousness and peace. As this bread is broken and shared among us this day, let us be filled with wisdom. As we take this bread, help us to be worthy and wise, fitting to celebrate Jesus Christ's death and resurrection in this special way. Amen.

PRAYER FOR THE CUP: How often, dear God, do we want to follow you, but only in our own way. We want discipleship when it is easy and commitment when it is convenient. Like Peter and the others, we back away when the Christ speaks to us of losing lives or taking up crosses. The cup we now lift for your blessing reminds us of our Savior's ultimate commitment for us. As we drink from it, let us grow in our commitment to Jesus, the living Christ. Through your Spirit we pray. Amen.

UNIFIED PRAYER: Be our wisdom, Lord, and our guide. As we gather at this table, feed us with mercy and peace. Help us to lead lives of righteousness and unity. Guide us to be humble, putting others first. You, in your wisdom, gave your Son for us to die and be born to life eternal. Let the nourishment we receive from taking this bread and cup strengthen us to do your will, telling others about your love. Fill us with the Holy Spirit, ready to share the wonderful message of our Savior, Jesus Christ. Amen.

PRAYER AFTER COMMUNION: At this table, Lord, we have drawn near to you. We feel your presence here. As we depart, go with us into the world, guiding our lives with wisdom. Amen.

Proper 21
Sunday between September 25 and October 1*

Esther 7:1–6, 9–10; 9:20–22
Psalm 124
James 5:13–20
Mark 9:38–50

PRAYER FOR THE BREAD: Gracious and redeeming God, in times of trouble you have always been with us. You have created heaven and earth, yet you care for us in our deepest needs. In Jesus Christ, we have looked upon your goodness and have been received as your children, even as your friends. In this bread we now bless and eat, we affirm this mystery: that you were once in our midst in human flesh and are even now in our midst by the power of your Spirit. Bless us as we partake, and let the living Christ work in us and through us. Amen.

PRAYER FOR THE CUP: God of compassion and mercy, you have always cared for your people. Through Jesus Christ, you have taught us the way of compassion, so we know through him that a cup of cold water given to another is an act that you bless. Even more, we remember that Jesus Christ loved us so much that he poured out his life for us. As we drink this cup, we confess that the Christ, whose life was poured out for us, is now the risen Lord, who reigns in glory. We pray that by your Spirit's guidance we will go from this place to pour out our love for others in true and humble service. Amen.

*When October 1 is a Sunday, refer to Prayers of Proper 22 for World Communion Sunday.

UNIFIED PRAYER: Dear God, hear us as we come to you in prayer. We are a sinful, weak, and self-centered people, and we ask that you work within our hearts to transform us into loving and caring people. Help us learn the power of prayer, both for our own needs and the needs of other people. At this communion table, help us learn from your love. May the bread we eat and the wine we drink bind us together as your people. May it strengthen us to move beyond our selfish needs so that we may give of ourselves to one another, as Christ gave himself for us. Open our hearts and eyes that we may realize the presence and power of Christ's Spirit in our midst and in our daily lives. Amen.

PRAYER AFTER COMMUNION: We have received from you, O giving God, food for our spirits, refreshment for our souls. Help us go from this place ready to bring refreshment and help to others in the world around us. Amen.

Proper 22
Sunday between October 2 and 8
(World Communion Sunday)

Job 1:1; 2:1–10
Psalm 26
Hebrews 1:1–4; 2:5–12
Mark 10:2–16

PRAYER FOR THE BREAD:

Creator of us all, as we partake of this bread let us remember that the body of Christ was broken for all—

For North and South Americans, Europeans, Asians, Australians, for all people around the globe.

The body of Christ was broken for the differently abled and the abled, for the rich and poor, for gay and straight.

The body of Christ was broken for those with shelter and street people, for those in prison and for those who are free, for the powerful and the powerless.

The body of Christ was broken for the liberal and conservative, for those on drugs and those who are drug free.

The body of Christ was broken for us all.

Let us celebrate and welcome all to this table.

In the name of Christ, who invites each of you to partake of this bread, we pray.*

PRAYER FOR THE CUP: God of time and eternity, you have sent us your son Jesus Christ to reflect your glory and to

*Contributed by Maureen Osuga; originally prayed at the assembly communion service at the Pittsburgh General Assembly of the Christian Church (Disciples of Christ), 1995.

purify us from our sins. Although superior to angels, he became human and accepted the way of the cross that we might also become your children. The cup we drink now recalls that sacrifice, the blood that sealed the new covenant for us. The cup we drink helps us recall that in this covenant you have called together people of all nations, that we truly drink it with all the world. Accept our praise and love. Speak to us through your Spirit. Amen.

UNIFIED PRAYER: Loving parent God, through Jesus Christ you have invited us to come to you as children. You call us to put aside our power and pretense, our dignity and defenses, so that we might open ourselves in awe and wonder to the mystery of what Christ has done for us. The bread we break and the cup we drink bring us into the presence of that mystery and the power of your presence. As we come to your table, bless us now as Jesus blessed the children. Fill our hearts with awe and joy at knowing we are in your presence. Guide us by your Spirit on the path that leads to your reign. In Christ's name we pray. Amen.

PRAYER AFTER COMMUNION: On this World Communion Sunday we have come as part of the whole people of God to gather at your table. We have taken bread and cup with brothers and sisters from all around this planet, gathered in your love and unified in your praise. Let the meaning of this moment expand our vision of what it means to be your one people in Jesus Christ. Amen.

Proper 23
Sunday between October 9 and 15
Job 23:1–9, 16–17
Psalm 22:1–15
Hebrews 4:12–16
Mark 10:17–31

PRAYER FOR THE BREAD: Through Jesus Christ you have given us the ability to approach your throne boldly, O Holy God. Through Jesus Christ we have discovered that you are a God of grace, a God of mercy. Bless the bread we now eat as a sign of that grace and mercy. Guide us by your Spirit in the paths of faith, that we might ever draw closer to you. Amen.

PRAYER FOR THE CUP: God of eternal love, we have heard your word for us, we have sung your praise, we have opened our hearts in prayer. Now we gather at your table to drink this cup. As we lift this cup for your blessing, let us find in it a sign of your compassion, a reminder of the lifeblood of Jesus Christ that was poured out for us. As we drink this cup, help us to remember that because Christ died, we live. Help us also to realize that we worship a living Christ, who gives us the power of life. We pray that you will dedicate us to be your loving, serving people. Amen.

UNIFIED PRAYER: Loving God, you are there for us in all the times of our lives. You are there in the joyous times and the sad times, the easy times and the hurting times. When we come to times when we are tested, help us to remember Jesus Christ, who bore a greater burden than we ever could, yet remained faithful. At this communion table, we eat the bread and drink the cup that help us to recall Christ's saving work. May your spirit of encouragement work in our midst as we partake, so we might be faithful to you as you are faithful to us. Amen.

PRAYER AFTER COMMUNION: Thank you, dear God, for this time of communion. Thank you, that in bread and wine we have drawn closer together to one another and to you. We pray now that this time of communion may transform our daily lives so that we may serve you by serving others. Amen.

Proper 24
Sunday between October 16 and 22

Job 38:1–7 (34–41)
Psalm 104:1–9, 24, 35c
Hebrews 5:1–10
Mark 10:35–45

PRAYER FOR THE BREAD: In wisdom you have made all your works, O God! What a great variety of creatures you have made! We are amazed at how you provide for all of life, how you meet the needs of all creatures. Here at this table we receive the bread of life, and here we recognize that you meet our deepest needs in Jesus Christ. Nourish our spirits and strengthen our souls. Nourish and strengthen this congregation and your church everywhere. Dedicate us to your purposes and lead us by your Spirit, that we may do your will. Amen.

PRAYER FOR THE CUP: Dear God, as we come to this table, forgive us for all we do that would disrupt community. Forgive us for pushing our own agendas at the expense of our brothers and sisters. Teach us the ways of servanthood and humility as we sit at the table here with Christ Jesus, for these are the ways of peace and wholeness. As we drink from the cup that reminds us of the sacrifice Christ made, give us the grace and courage to drink from the cup of discipleship as well. Support us with your Spirit in our efforts to be faithful. Amen.

UNIFIED PRAYER: We bless you, Creator God, for you are clothed with honor and majesty. Galaxies and thunderclouds bear your signature. Life springs abundant because you have willed it. And yet you are a gentle God. In tender mercy you reach out to heal your people. You bless the meek and the poor in spirit. You sent your Son, Jesus Christ, to be among us as a servant. At this table we break bread and drink from the cup to honor the one who would teach us the way of servanthood and kindness. Help us here to move beyond our pride and defensiveness to allow Christ's Spirit to work within us and among us. Amen.

PRAYER AFTER COMMUNION:

Too soon we rise; the symbols disappear;
the feast, though not the love, is past and gone;
the bread and wine remove, but thou art here—
nearer than ever—still our shield and sun.*

*Horatius Bonar, "Here, O My Lord, I See Thee Face to Face," alt.

Proper 25
Sunday between October 23 and 29

Job 42:1–6, 10–17
Psalm 34:1–8 (19–22)
Hebrews 7:23–28
Mark 10:46–52

PRAYER FOR THE BREAD: You love us as we are, dear God, but you invite us to live transformed lives. You accept us in our brokenness, dear God, but you offer us the chance to accept healing and forgiveness. You have invited us to this table, dear God, not because you owe us favors, but because you are gracious and loving. The bread that we break reminds us that your son, Jesus, came to earth in human form and that he offered his life for our sake. As we eat this bread, renew our spirits so that we may faithfully follow the paths of discipleship. Amen.

PRAYER FOR THE CUP: Gracious God, we come to you because in Jesus Christ we have seen your loving face. We come to you because Jesus Christ has reconciled us to you and called us into a new and loving relationship with you and with our neighbors. May this cup we drink be a sign of that new and loving relationship. As we drink it, draw us ever closer to you and to one another. Bless us with the presence of your Spirit. Amen.

UNIFIED PRAYER: In a world of distracting influences, hype, loud noise, and bright lights, we are often blind to your presence, creator God. We think so much about our own wants and desires, our own fears and concerns, that we forget that you are the one who created us and that you are the one who calls us to faith. Let us, like Bartimaeus, have the faith to call upon Christ's name and the desire to find health and wholeness in Christ's word. Let the silence of this communion service be a time when we can call upon you and listen for your call to us. Let the bread that we break and the cup that we bless help us remember the Christ who came that we might have life and wholeness. Bless us with the presence of your Spirit in our lives, that in the confusion of our everday existence we may find the calm and peace that only you can give. Amen.

PRAYER AFTER COMMUNION: May the peace of God, the love of God, and the power of God that we have experienced here continue to grow in our lives, that others may experience God's love through us. Amen.

Proper 26
Sunday between October 30 and November 5

Ruth 1:1–18
Psalm 146
Hebrews 9:11–14
Mark 12: 28–34

PRAYER FOR THE BREAD: We praise you, loving God, and we find our hope in your love. It is you who made sky and stars, land and sea. It is you who brings justice for the oppressed and who gives food to the hungry. We come now hungry in spirit, asking for the bread that only you can give. The physical bread that we eat is but a symbol of that living bread, Jesus Christ, who nourishes our souls. Bless us as we gather here as one family in Christ, and guide us by your Spirit that we may be a blessing to others. Amen.

PRAYER FOR THE CUP: We worship you, O living God! We praise your name. You have loved us, you have formed us, and you have called us to be your people. We now gather to bless this cup and to give you thanks for Jesus Christ our Lord. In drinking this cup, we acknowledge that Christ offered a sacrifice with his own blood for our eternal redemption. Let us realize in a deeper way than we have before the significance of Christ's gift to us. Transform our lives with your Spirit, so that we may live, witness, and love in such a way that the world will recognize us as your redeemed people. Amen.

UNIFIED PRAYER: We come together, dear God, to remember and to learn from Jesus Christ. We realize that this service of communion is a time when we reenact the love that Jesus had for his disciples, and a time when we celebrate the love that the living Christ has for us. Bless this loaf and bless this cup with your love. Transform our hearts and spirits as we partake, so that we may allow your love to work within us. At this table, we recognize that we are more than a group of individuals; we are a community of faith. Draw us together to one another in your love, and teach us to love others as you love us. And help us realize that the love you give us is not meant to be contained within this community but is to be shared with the world. Guide us by your Spirit that we may live out your love as Christ would have us do. Amen.

PRAYER AFTER COMMUNION: We have shared a sacred meal with Christ as our host, and we have experienced your love for us. Bless us as we go from this place, and help us to recognize and put into action opportunities to love others in your name. Amen.

Proper 27
Sunday between November 6 and 12

>*Ruth 3:1–5; 4:13–17*
>*Psalm 127*
>*Hebrews 9:24–28*
>*Mark 12:38–44*

PRAYER FOR THE BREAD: Each time we come to your table, Lord, help us to reflect how we worship you. It is not the showy and glittering edifices that we have built that count; it is not the loud or solemn music that pleases you. It is not our fine clothes and pious attitudes. We worship you best as we humbly give all we are able with our lives and gifts. As this bread is broken, we know it represents the ultimate sacrifice from you, the body of your Son, Jesus Christ. Help us to give ourselves to you in worship and in all our lives. Amen.

PRAYER FOR THE CUP: God of glory, we come today wanting to be your faithful people. We are clever, wealthy, powerful, and technologically advanced in so many ways, yet we know that you do not measure us by such standards. May this time of communion be a time when we begin to grow in spirit, in compassion, in generosity, and in true humility. For the cup from which we drink reminds us that our Lord Jesus Christ is the one we call teacher. Help us learn Christ's ways through the grace of your Spirit. Amen.

UNIFIED PRAYER: In coming to this table today, O Gracious God, we confess that we do not always put you first in our lives. It is too easy for us to make other priorities, leaving for you what time and money is left over. Yet, your Son, Jesus Christ, was sacrificed once and for all because of your great love for us. You gave your only Son to us in your generosity. Let this bread and cup remind us of your great gift. Help us to live lives that reflect that you are our foundation. Amen.

PRAYER AFTER COMMUNION: We have gathered at your table, dear God, in this sanctuary. We have known Christ's presence here. May we remember that Jesus Christ is our true sanctuary, not made with human hands, not limited to one time or place. May every time we share bread with one another be a time when we know Christ's presence. Amen.

PROPER 28
Sunday between November 13 and 19

1 Samuel 1:4–20
1 Samuel 2:1–10
Hebrews 10:11–14 (15–18), 19–25
Mark 13:1–8

PRAYER FOR THE BREAD: God of surprises, you have the power to turn cries of anguish and need into songs of joy. We so often feel trapped and devalued in this sometimes harsh and judgmental world. Help us to find at this communion table a place where we are loved for who we are, your children. As we eat this bread that helps us to remember Christ's sacrifice for us, nourish us and strengthen us so that we may sing your praises and bless your name. Amen.

PRAYER FOR THE CUP: God of purity and light, Jesus Christ has given us the confidence that we need to come before you. Christ has opened the way for us to enter into your presence. By the power of Christ, cleanse our hearts and purify our minds. We thank you for this cup that symbolizes the sacrifice that Christ made for us. Help us to hold fast to the faith to which we have been called, to trust in the promises we have received through Jesus Christ. Amen.

UNIFIED PRAYER: God of grace and mercy, we thank you for this church building in which we gather and all the memories and associations it brings to our minds. Yet we realize that this building in itself is not the church. We realize that we are part of a temple not made with hands and that Jesus Christ is our cornerstone. We are part of a church made not of brick and mortar, but of human beings drawn together by Christ's love. Let this bread and wine help us to remember Jesus Christ and to affirm his presence in our midst. As we bless, serve, and consume these elements, give us the strength, courage, and love so that we might truly be Christ's body. Amen.

PRAYER AFTER COMMUNION: You have called us; we came. You have fed us; we have partaken. Now as you send us, O God of the prophets, help us to witness to your name, live by your Spirit, and walk the paths of justice and compassion. Amen.

Proper 29
Sunday between November 20 and 26
(Reign of Christ Sunday)

> 2 Samuel 23:1–7
> Psalm 132:1–12, (13–18)
> Revelation 1:4b–8
> John 18:33–37

PRAYER FOR THE BREAD: Many seek our allegiance and obedience, God, and promise us many rewards in return. Yet at our baptism, we accepted Christ as our Lord and Savior. Help us be true to that commitment. Help us to be faithful to Christ as we break this bread, remembering that Christ gave his own body for our sakes. Help us to faithfully follow the paths of love as your Spirit guides us. Amen.

PRAYER FOR THE CUP: The Christ we follow was dressed not in rich, fine garments, but in a poor person's simple clothes. The Christ we follow drank not from the jeweled goblet of a king, but from a simple cup. The Christ we follow didn't lord it over others, but came as a servant. Yet, in drinking this cup, we affirm this Christ as ruler of our lives. Eternal God, forgive us when we stray from Christ's way, and call us back through your Spirit, so that we may give you glory forever. Amen.

UNIFIED PRAYER: In Jesus Christ you have revealed yourself to us, O God, as the Alpha and the Omega, the beginning and the end, who was, and is, and is to come. We gather now at this table, seeking to share in communion with the one true God. In taking this bread, breaking it, and eating it, we affirm that you sent your son to earth as a human being, who offered himself for our sakes. In blessing this cup, sharing and drinking from it, we affirm that your love was poured out for us in Christ's sacrifice. May this self-giving, loving Christ reign in our hearts. Amen.

PRAYER AFTER COMMUNION: The Jesus who broke bread and lifted the cup in the upper room went on to face death on the cross. Yet, through the power of God, he rose from the dead and is now Lord of all. Thank you, gracious God, for having been able to break bread and lift the cup with the living Christ. Amen.

Scripture Index

Psalms

Isaiah

61:10—62:3	Christmas 1
62:6—12	Christmas Eve/Day
64:1—9	Advent 1

Jeremiah

31:7—14	Christmas 2
31:31—34	Lent 5

Ezekiel

37:1—14	Pentecost

Hosea

2:14—20	Epiphany 8, Proper 3

Jonah

3:1—5, 10	Epiphany 3

Mark

1:1—8	Advent 2
1:9—15	Lent 1
1:14—20	Epiphany 3
1:21—28	Epiphany 4
1:29—39	Epiphany 5
1:40—45	Epiphany 6, Proper 1
2:1—12	Epiphany 7, Proper 2
2:13—22	Epiphany 8, Proper 3
2:23—3:6	Last Sunday after Epiphany, Proper 4
3:20—35	Proper 5
4:26—34	Proper 6
4:35—41	Proper 7
5:21—43	Proper 8
6:1—13	Proper 9
6:14—29	Proper 10
6:30—34, 53—56	Proper 11
7:1—8, 14—15, 21—23	Proper 17
7:24—37	Proper 18
8:27—38	Proper 19
8:31—38	Lent 2
9:2—9	Last Sunday after Epiphany, Lent 2
9:30—37	Proper 20

John

Acts

Romans

1 Corinthians

2 Corinthians